Be ufictos!

Mln Nood

INFECTIOUS

HOW TO CONNECT DEEPLY AND UNLEASH THE ENERGETIC LEADER WITHIN

INFECTIOUS

HOW TO CONNECT DEEPLY AND UNLEASH THE ENERGETIC LEADER WITHIN

by Achim Nowak

ALLWORTH PRESS
NEW YORK

Allworth Press books may be purchased in bulk at special discounts for sales promotion, corporate gifts, fund-raising, or educational purposes. Special editions can also be created to specifications. For details, contact the Special Sales Department, Allworth Press, 307 West 36th Street, 11th Floor, New York, NY 10018 or info@skyhorsepublishing.com.

15 14 13 12 11   5 4 3 2 1

Published by Allworth Press, an imprint of Skyhorse Publishing, Inc.307 West 36th Street, 11th Floor, New York, NY 10018.Allworth Press® is a registered trademark of Skyhorse Publishing, Inc.®, a Delaware corporation.

www.allworth.com

Cover design by Brian Peterson

Library of Congress Cataloging-in-Publication Data is available on file.

ISBN: 978-1-58115-924-0

Printed in the United States of America

Contents

Don't play what's there. Play what's not there . . .

Miles Davis

Introduction

Consider this.

At a cocktail party, five executives engage in chitchat with each other and assorted guests. It is a very typical kind of affair. Hors d'oeuvres and martinis and harmless social banter. Entirely unexceptional. Three days later the same executives appear, one at a time, before a panel of judges to present a business plan. The winning plan will be fully financed by a team of venture capitalists. Alex "Sandy" Pentland and Daniel Olguín, researchers at the MIT Human Dynamics Lab, closely monitor the behavior of the five executives at the cocktail party. Without reading or hearing their pitches to the panel, without any inkling at all of what the executives will propose, they forecast who will present the winning plan.

Accurately, of course.

Powerful stuff, I think to myself. So what the heck did Pentland and Olguín monitor? They outfitted the executives with devices that recorded data on their social signals—not what they said, but their tone of voice, gesticulation, proximity to others, personal energy, and more. All that is not spoken. Pentland and Olguín call these unspoken signals honest signals.[1] A biological term, *honest signals* refers to the nonverbal cues that social species use to coordinate themselves—gestures, expressions, tone. Humans are unusual in that their honest signals will cause changes in the receiver. Clear, biological changes. When asked in an interview in *Harvard Business Review* which kind of honest signals are most clearly identified with successful people, Pentland's answer was emphatic: "The more successful people are more energetic."[2]

So what do I do, you may ask? Turn on my energy faucet a little more?

Let me take you to another event. On a balmy November evening, 800 people cram into the hulking Chapman Conference Room at Miami Dade College in downtown Miami. Several hundred others hover outside the doors, waiting in vain to claim a seat. A languid autumn breeze wafts through the building's courtyard, and yet there is a current of excitement in the air. The occasion? Nobel Prize–winning author Orhan Pamuk is the featured guest at The Miami International Book Fair, and folks have come to see and hear him.

When Mr. Pamuk takes the stage he recounts his evolution as a writer and reads from his latest novel, *The Museum of Innocence*. My friend Letty Bassart and I sit in the tenth row. The moment Mr. Pamuk starts to read I suddenly connect with memories of my childhood, part of it spent in Istanbul, the setting of his book. I connect with memories of the 1970s, the period in which the main action of the book occurs. I connect with the characters as they navigate their way through sexual exploration and first love. I connect with things I had not contemplated for quite a long time. I connect, if you will, with parts of myself that I had temporarily forgotten.

A few minutes into Mr. Pamuk's reading, Letty gives me a nudge. We look at the audience around us and marvel. Folks are sitting with their bodies lurching forward. Heads cupped in their hands. Eyes closed to better absorb the words. Arms reaching for a loved one sitting next to them. The body language of intense engagement is all around us. At the same time this physical spell is imbued with a remarkable stillness. There is an absence of rustling and nervous coughing and buttocks shifting in seats. The energy in the room is palpable, as if it could be touched. It is the sort of energy that comes with rapt attention and surrender.

Irony has it, the moment Mr. Pamuk uttered his first words I noticed his accent. Mr. Pamuk's command of the English language is impeccable, but English is clearly not his native tongue. When he reads from his book, he reads the English words as translated by someone else, not the original Turkish words he wrote. And since we are in Miami, most members of the audience around us do not claim English as their first language, either. It doesn't matter. Connection is a gift that happens in a realm other than words. The imagination of the author stirs our imagination, well beyond the literal meaning of language. We connect at the level of all that is human, universal, timeless. We connect at the level of the cellular and the unspoken.

The event with Orhan Pamuk lasts 90 minutes at best, but Letty and I leave feeling immensely satisfied. Stirred. Alive. And yes—dare I say it—strangely connected to all of the other book lovers around us.

A reading is a formal event, of course. Roles are defined. The author shows up with the intent to communicate, and the audience comes with the intent to receive the communication. Yet we all have attended equally formal events where we couldn't wait to bolt out of the room. What made this a memorable evening? Was it the beauty of Mr. Pamuk's writing? The collective curiosity of the audience? Each of these elements no doubt contributed to the unfolding of this delicious event. But the real connectors, of this I am certain, were all the intangible qualities that emanated from Mr. Pamuk. His inexorable charm. His wit, his warm personal energy. More so than the seductiveness of his writing,

Mr. Pamuk himself was the conduit that created the possibility of connection.

CONNECTABILITY IS MISSION CRITICAL

Why does Mr. Pamuk's ability to connect matter? Well, I trust that Mr. Pamuk's skill as a personal connector instantly caused a spike in his book sales that evening. The line of folks waiting for him to autograph their books ringed all the way around the back of the conference center and spilled out into the lobby. Increased book sales benefit Mr. Pamuk personally and make his publisher happy. But more importantly, they help him to affect more readers, touch more people, and create connections that reach well beyond the ephemeral experience of this Friday night. They magnify his impact on the world.

Here's how the connection conversation unfolds in my firm. The most common request we receive goes something like this: "Marjorie is a Senior VP and one of our brightest stars. She is highly respected by all of her colleagues. But Marjorie lacks executive presence. Can you help her?" *Executive presence* is a marvelous code word that encapsulates a lot of unspoken signals and messages. In plain English, it boils down to this: Marjorie doesn't engage or inspire folks. Her energy doesn't spark the imagination of others. In high-stakes situations, Marjorie fails to connect.

The other request we often hear is a little more direct: "Ricardo is really bright and a great asset to our company. But people who work for him get frustrated with his rambling style and lack of clarity. Eventually they just tune out. Can you help him be more effective?" This inquiry is commonly framed as a need to tweak a person's communication style. That is, in many instances, accomplished with relative ease. What is almost never said, however, is what lies beneath: Ricardo doesn't connect with people, and they certainly do not connect with him.

For anyone who wishes to succeed in business—whether you're an entrepreneur building your own company or a professional in a large corporation—the ability to connect is vital. Not just vital—essential, mission critical. Without it, every one of us eventually hits the glass ceiling. Glass ceilings exist in nearly every aspect of business life. Connectability—the ease and consistency with which we connect with others—is the least talked about yet in many ways most daunting of these ceilings.

It never fails. When I receive the phone call for help, I am not asked to assist the professional who somehow fails to generate results. No, it is invariably because a fast-rising superstar has hit this ceiling. More often than not it is the high producer: the one who excelled at school; the one who can outsmart the rest of the team at the drop of a dime. His inability to meaningfully connect in high-level business situations suddenly becomes the deal-breaker. The first time it happens is the moment when everything suddenly turns. When being very good at what he does isn't good enough anymore.

Mind you, I am not talking about your personality, your likeability, your manners, or the constellations of your Myers-Briggs-Type-Indicator profile. They are all a part of this conversation, yes—but just a very, very small part. We are simply talking about the ability to forge a resonant connection with another human being. HR professionals do not like to talk about this. Connectability doesn't show up on performance reviews. It is deemed too difficult to quantify. "The inability to forge collaborative relationships" is as close as we get to describing the problem. Yes, we have created lots of code language to dance around this pretty self-evident truth: Individuals who know how to consistently connect get rewarded. Individuals who don't—well, they are shipped to the expert graveyard. They don't get called back for the second interview, in spite of their exceptional qualifications. They don't get the promotion they have worked so hard to earn. They simply aren't invited to the party.

OUR HABITS INHIBIT CONNECTION

Here's the vicious part about connecting: All of us operate within a confounding cultural paradox. At work, we spend more and more of our time communicating with people. We have access to technology that accelerates our ability to reach others. We complain about the amount of emails we send and receive. We attend one mandatory meeting after another—in person, via phone. We talk pretty much nonstop. Add to this what we do in our private lives. A recent study by the Pew Research Center found that half of American teenagers—the next generation of our workforce—send 50 or more text messages a day, and that one-third sends more than a 100 a day.[3] Two-thirds of the teen texters interviewed by the center asserted that they were, in fact, more likely to use their cell phones to text friends than to call them.

We're busy doing lots of communicating. Lots and lots of it.

Top this off with the fact that we grown-ups have been trained to speak in corporate-speak that doesn't offend. We have attended business writing classes that teach us to be concise. We abhor emails that get detailed. Much of our daily communication is reduced to the exchange of quick bits of information. We have stripped communication down to its bare bones.

We communicate at a furious pace—yet we connect less and less.

I believe that, at times, a routine conversation about absolutely nothing can be very satisfying. In that moment, with that particular person, it may be all I desire. I believe just as strongly, however, that a deep, spine-tingling connection is an inherently good thing. I believe that it is an age-old, primordial experience. I believe that such a connection creates good feelings in us and in others. It accelerates our success in the world. I also believe that in an increasingly complex world, circumstances conspire against genuine connection while connection becomes more critical than ever. Something that a generation ago seemed simple doesn't seem so simple anymore.

REMEMBERING THE POSSIBLE

Sometimes we get lucky and we stumble into a moment that gives us the proverbial goose bumps. Such a moment reminds us of how simple a connection really is—and how we can feel it in every part of our body.

I remember a drive I took with Ane and Baba—my mom and dad—on the German Autobahn, sometime in the spring of 2002. Germany is the country where I was born, and this was a quintessentially gray German morning, the sky hanging low with thick, lumpy clouds. I was returning from a pilgrimage to see one of my spiritual teachers, Mother Meera, and Ane and Baba were chauffeuring me back to the Frankfurt airport. We sat in the car, and we chatted about absolutely nothing as we headed down the Autobahn from Limburg. It was, in fact, an utterly ordinary drive. Yet, as I sat in the backseat of their old '93 Mercedes, I felt a delicious sense of peace and calm. Waves of joy washed over my body. It is hard to put it into words, but somehow my body knew that for this moment all was well in the world, that this ride with Ane and Baba was the most perfect ride that could unfold just then. The faded brown leather of the car seats, the scratched veneer of the formica dashboard, the curled up carpet at the tip of my shoes—they all seemed to vibrate with a flickering energy. Everything, and every one of us in the car, was touched by this energy. It was as if all of our molecules were plugged into one large cosmic power outlet.

Such moments with my parents were a rare occurrence; that's why I remember this ride so well. When I strip away the outer circumstances of that particular morning, I am left with this: Locked in that old Mercedes of theirs, Ane and Baba and I were, in a way, returning to an original state of being. A state of ease with others. A state where connectedness is tactile, vibratory, and enormously satisfying. Where, within every fiber of our being, it feels darn good.

What if we actually knew how to make such spine-tingling moments happen? What if such moments were not mere lucky accidents? Better yet, what if we could make them happen in our business relationships, day in, day out?

FOUR LEVELS OF CONNECTION

Here's what I know: Folks who connect really well connect on four levels. These four levels move from the visible to the invisible realm, from the surface to the core, from the small moment to the cosmic one. We all play on all of these levels all the time. Thing is, most of us don't play with any measure of consciousness. We don't play the levels, the levels play us. They define every interaction we have.

At times, this may work nicely. Just as I did during my car ride with Ane and Baba, we all stumble into the occasional moment of grace. Often, we connect on just one or two of the levels. That's fine. But when we habitually don't play well on one or several of the levels, we actively inhibit connection. We do so, day in and day

4 Levels of Connection

Talk

Power

Intent

Energy

Table 1: What we put out to the world

out. We always run smack up against our own glass ceiling. We never get to the infectious connections—not even the accidental ones.

In *Infectious*, we will immerse ourselves in exploring the Four Levels of Connection (Table 1). I will make each level as accessible as I can for you. I hope that as you explore the pages of this book, you will find, at each level, concrete tools that will assist you in fine-tuning the way you engage with others. This is the work I do with my cherished business clients. In the pages that follow I place all of my tools at your fingertips. Try them out. Explore. And please, have fun!

LEVEL ONE IS THE TALK LEVEL

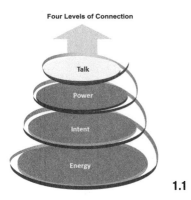

1.1

We have been told that creating a connection depends on our ability to have a conversation. That's what is taught in corporate communication programs and, if you are fortunate, your university. How we ask questions, how we listen. If you studied neuro-linguistic programming, you learned the advanced version of this material: how to notice and match the communication signals of those with whom you engage. Good stuff. The folks I coach, however, know this and are often still not as compelling as they would like to be in a one-on-one chat. So I have reduced surface conversation skills down to five very, very simple principles. Of this I am certain: These principles work. They are simple, and that is their beauty. When we apply them with rigor, they make a palpable difference in how we show up and how others experience us.

Pentland and Olguín clearly show us that what we say is only a tiny portion of our personal impact. Agreed—but a lack of finesse at the Talk Level is a deal-breaker in any conversation. When we don't play well at this first level, we never get to taste the richer levels of connection.

LEVEL TWO IS THE POWER LEVEL

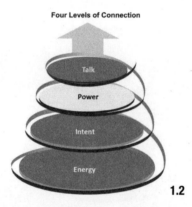

1.2

I remember how I felt when Reverend Mona called me a doormat. Well, it really pissed me off! I was on a six-week-long personal discovery retreat in Rimrock, Arizona, and it was the first time in my life I had taken time off to look at myself. I was in my mid-thirties, a successful theater director in New York, recognized for my work. Very sure that I was "somebody." Cocky, and at the same time also full of doubts. Then, Reverend Mona, the facilitator of my desert experience, had the audacity to call me a doormat. How dare she?

Once I stopped reeling from Mona's remark, I quickly began to see all the ways in which I was not very powerful at all. I realized that I had no idea what personal power actually was. I certainly did not know how to channel it in a manner that might fortify my connection with others.

People who connect well have a conscious and helpful relationship with their own power. They also play well with the power of others. They enjoy power rather than fear it. We will break the experience of power into five power plugs that we can turn to—and turn on. These plugs recharge the quality of our connection with anyone we meet.

If we don't know how to invoke our personal power, our connection with others will always be impaired. We will show up with a diminished self—which in turn, diminishes the potential connection with anyone else. If we are willful creatures we'll don the alter ego of the diminished self—grandiosity. It matters little; the outcome will be the same.

LEVEL THREE IS THE INTENT LEVEL

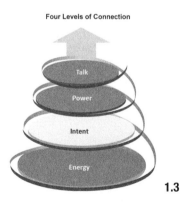

Four Levels of Connection

Talk

Power

Intent

Energy

1.3

It's one of the first things an actor learns in acting class. When I learn my lines, I don't just say the lines, I play the objective.

The objective defines the impact my character wishes to have on another character. A clear objective changes the way words flow out of my mouth; it sharpens their focus and impact. It heightens the reality of a scene, makes it crackle and shine.

And this is the beauty of an objective: It is silent. It lives in my brain and is my little secret—but it so brazenly changes the way every moment plays out.

Intent is the everyday-language equivalent of an actor's objective. Great connectors show up alert, with awareness and clear purpose. They don't just fall into conversations, they help shape them with conscious intent. What fun!

We will examine three different aspects of intent as we dissect this third level of connection. Conscious intent will shape the impact I have on another person. Conscious intent may define the tone of the encounter I have with another person. And conscious intent will show up in the social role I choose to play.

If this still sounds a little abstract, never fear. It is great fun to explore intent and discover how it instantly changes our encounters with others. But beware: Our Four Levels of Connection are—pardon the pun—interconnected. When we don't play well at the Talk and Power levels, our Intent will be thwarted and derailed.

LEVEL FOUR IS THE ENERGY LEVEL

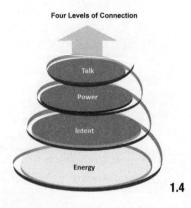

Four Levels of Connection

Talk

Power

Intent

Energy

1.4

I saved the best for last—even though it is often the first thing we notice in a person. Energy is the heart and soul level at which connections either do or do not happen. Without personal energy—energy that vibrates within us and viscerally touches others—our ability to connect will always be constrained. Without such energy, every social effort will be reduced to a more or less routine exchange. It will lack spark, flow, dimension. It will be— arrrgh!—forgettable. My goal is to demystify the often mystifying experience of energy for us. We will look at how we access our energy. Contain energy. Release it. Remove energy blocks. And play with the energy that others send our way.

Great personal energy alone, however, is just that: great personal energy. We may admire it. We may even be uplifted by it. If it is to have form and impact, it needs to be supported by our ease with the preceding three levels. Infectious connections happen in that magical moment when the conversation skills, sense of personal power, intent, and energy of two people converge. I am sure you can remember a moment when you were speaking with someone who spoke well and had interesting things to say, who looked comfortable in her own skin, seemed to really want to talk with you, and whose personal energy was—well, infectious. If, in that same conversation, you also spoke well and had interesting things to say, were comfortable in your own skin, truly wanted to speak with that person, and were bursting with personal energy . . . wow, what an amazing conversation that must have been. I sure would have enjoyed being a fly on that wall!

You will find many tools in *Infectious* that you can put to practice immediately. Any small change you make in how you play in any of the levels of connection will affect the dynamic of a relationship, be it professional or personal. Before we start to tinker around with the tools, however, let us examine some common misconceptions about social conduct. I think of these misconceptions as the hidden rules to which we have never agreed but which we nevertheless follow, every day. They are pervasive and persistent, and they really get in our way. They are limiting beliefs—and really now, why the heck would we wish to limit ourselves when it comes to connecting with a fellow human being?

Chapter 1

Stop the Fake Conversations

"I hate business dinners," George Brinkman says to me. He says it with a ferocious conviction, and I am startled by the intensity of his comment. George is a seasoned business executive, a sharp guy with a keen mind. Funny, dry. The sort of fellow whose thoughts are always three steps ahead of everyone else's. George speaks well and uses language beautifully. And his senior role at a Fortune 500 company requires him to attend lots and lots of such dinners.

"I hate the moment when we run out of things to say," George adds. There's a long, pregnant pause. "And that moment always comes . . ."

Hmm, I think to myself. What I really dislike is not the dinners—no, it's the fake conversations. They leave me feeling empty, and they zap the life out of me. I have a hunch these are the conversations George is talking about. The sports/weather/favorite TV show/happy family conversations. The blah blah blah of predictable chatter. The blah blah blah of no surprises. The blah blah blah of just filling up time with easy narratives. You have been there. You know.

Behind each of these conversations lurk some pretty powerful beliefs that drive how we approach another person and engage them. Some are clear and up front in our conscious mind. They likely hail from the worlds in which we grew up—our immediate family and the cultural norms into which we were born—and they explicitly inform what we say, what we don't say, the energy we use to engage, the social etiquette we follow or don't follow.

There's a whole other range of beliefs that we likely cannot put into words. They hover in our subconscious mind—and that, of course, is their danger. They are not known to us, yet they write the script we follow. Couple this with the fact that everyone else is following their unspoken scripts, and the story suddenly becomes pretty complicated. All of us operate within a powerful collective consciousness which defines how we seek to connect with others—and much of this consciousness is not conscious. And so it happens again. We sit down for a meal, and suddenly we're adrift in yet another fake conversation.

Blah. Blah. Blah. Blah. Blah. Blah. Yes, it just goes on.

Let us name some of these beliefs that inhabit our conscious and subconscious minds. Here are my top five. There are more, of course—but these five beliefs alone are powerful threads in our social storylines. We may not be aware of them, but they present barriers to a genuine connection.

BELIEF #1: FIND COMMON GROUND—FAST.

You have talked to him before. He impresses you because he speaks so well. He may have worked in sales for a while. He showers you with unwavering eye contact. Every question he sends your way is a missile seeking common ground. And any answer you offer—and I mean any— will be twisted into a shared narrative. Like it or not, he will pin you into a common-ground storyline.

Doesn't sound so bad, does it?

Here's a conversation I have nearly every week. Since I am originally from Germany and have a foreign-sounding name, a first conversation with pretty much anyone quickly settles on Germany as a topic. This often means that my new acquaintance tells me about a trip she took to Germany, a place she visited, and lavishly praises the things she appreciates or loves about my country of origin. Makes sense, right?

The underlying assumption is that I value Germany just as much as she does. Truth is, I have a bunch of ambivalent thoughts and feelings about Germany. That's why I live in South Florida and not in Cologne or Munich. A nuanced conversation about things I value or don't value about Germany, or the not-so-simple feelings many expats have about their countries of origin, would interest me. However, when I offer a comment like, "You know, after a week in Germany I'm really ready to come home," or, "The longer I'm away from Germany, the more I believe that most of the stereotypes are true," our conversation about Germany tends to come to a crashing halt. I have violated the assumption that we share similar views about a seemingly safe topic. The common-ground storyline no longer holds.

My comments could, of course, be heard as an invitation to a richer conversation. Questions like, "Why do you choose to live in the United States?" or, "Is there anything you miss about Germany?" or, "What do you enjoy most when you visit Germany?" might steer our chat in a surprising direction. These questions rarely come in a first chat.

This is what the missile is truly aiming for: Common ground means you will like me. You will not feel uncomfortable. More importantly, common ground means I won't feel uncomfortable. We will have a pleasant and neatly bound conversation. And, yes, it will remain ever so predictable and fake.

Common ground is, in many ways, a wonderful thing. The singular quest to find it, however, is not. It puts a tremendous strain on a conversation. I remember a round of frequent conversations where my ability to find commonality was sorely put to the test. In the early 1990s, I spent several years working with junior and senior high school students throughout the New York City public school system, training them to become mediators. A basic mediation training lasted three days, and during those three days there were ample opportunities to bond with my trainees. Invariably our conversations would turn to the sorts of music we liked. This was initially always an awkward moment for me. Many of my students liked the latest rap or hip-hop artists. I tended to switch the dial on the radio when "that" music came on. It was not the kind of music I enjoyed at all! I found it quite impossible to have an excited conversation about my students' favorite music.

Well, I quickly decided to simply listen to their likes and then also talk about the kind of music I liked. At that time in my life, that was New Age and European trance music. These conversations often became much richer than if we actually liked the same music. It made us dig deep to explain what we liked about our music, how it made us feel, and why we chose to listen to it. How rewarding those conversations were!

The beauty of a conversation that delves a little deeper is this: While we may discover that we don't like the same music, we are able to better understand what we truly love about the music we do like. The common ground has suddenly been reframed. It is no longer about liking the same music—that is a very small frame, indeed. It is about our passion for music and how it makes us feel, which is a much wider and richer frame. The conversation has actually steered us toward a new common ground. While it may take us a while to get there, it is a common ground with resonance and depth—a common ground that has been earned.

Reality: *Common ground is wonderful when it is earned. Common ground is irrelevant when it is forced. Quick common ground banishes us to instantly forgettable connections. Take your time to discover common ground—and relish the many things that you do not have in common.*

BELIEF #2: AVOID CHARGED TOPICS.

Imagine the bubbly voice of Dr. Margarita Gurri, a Cuban-American psychologist and parent coach from Miami with a high-voltage personality. This is her story:

> As children in cotillion class, we were taught the social graces. Over several weeks, we would enter a room dressed in suit and tie or dress with heels and hose, ready to be polished socially. Mastering the social arts of introductions, table manners, dancing, and asking or being asked to dance was the task at hand. Socialite Hazel Nowakowski graciously demonstrated and actively coached children to enter society as socially responsible beings.
>
> Two of the prime directives stressed the importance of saying yes when asked to dance and making conversation. We were instructed to get to know someone by chatting about superficial topics, avoiding personal issues, politics, religion, finances, and—most of all—disagreements. We were encouraged to draw the other person out, talking about their interests, laughing at their jokes, and 'making them feel special.' The goal was genuine attentiveness without conflict.

Does cotillion class sound a little extreme to you? Is this an all-too-specific story of female indoctrination? A narrow glimpse at how upper-class Cubans in the US acculturate their own?

All true, perhaps. But take the cotillion part out of the story, and how many of us, deep down, ascribe to the same list of social dos that Margarita learned as a young girl?

My friend Philip Friday, for example, is an impeccable social animal. A well-bred gentleman from Savannah, Georgia, he is the living embodiment of many of Margarita's social lessons. Philip focuses intently on whomever he speaks with. He knows how to draw a person out. He makes every person feel special. His beaming energy melts the most obdurate conversation partner.

Yes, Philip's warmth is infectious. He is a master of the breezy social connection. It is quite remarkable; I watch in awe as people clamor to be around Philip. The shadow side of this make-them-feel-good, stay-away-from-anything-controversial approach? Philip knows lots and lots about other people. They know very little about him. His social skill creates the trompe l'oeil of a connection. A one-sided connection, that is.

Margarita makes it clear that she values what she learned from Mrs. Nowakowski's cotillion class. But such lessons are hugely detrimental in a contemporary business setting. Reduced to its essence, the message is this: When you talk, take no risks. Don't reveal yourself. Don't have a point of view. Hide behind the mask of easy social banter. Keep it light, light, light.

All of us know the old dictum about avoiding religion and politics when we chat at a social event. There is well-intentioned wisdom behind that advice, of course. But what sort of price do we pay when we habitually avoid topics on which we might disagree with others?

The decision to abandon Belief #2 is a powerful game-changer in any relationship. It instantly shifts the quality of every human connection we have. In the next chapter we'll look in depth at how we do this with a measure of skill. I know from the connections in my own world how powerful it is to break this code. I grew up in a nonreligious environment. As an adult, after years of exploring my spirituality, I have now settled into practicing Hinduism. I meditate. I chant in Sanskrit. I worship in an ashram filled with altars of Indian deities and holy people. For a long time, this was something I wouldn't mention while grabbing a drink with a colleague after work or chatting with a client at a formal business dinner. Truth is, I don't have a great need to talk about this part of my life, but nowadays, when a conversation steers into these waters, I will. Whenever I do, the relationship rewards—you guessed it—are tremendous. My willingness to reveal something intimate allows my colleague to do the same. We are able to surprise each other. How wonderful that is!

Reality: Breezy social banter helps to kill time in an airport lounge before the next drink arrives. It fosters the illusion of connection—a connection of little meaning and less value. In today's media-saturated world, being comfortable discussing current and controversial topics is critical. In business, having the confidence to disagree, explore points of conflict, and learn new points of view elevates the quality of our relationships.

BELIEF #3: DON'T SHOW THE CRACKS.

Stuart Perkins is a CEO who understands the power of the vulnerable moment.

In a meeting room tucked away in the bowels of the Chicago O'Hare Hilton, Stuart addresses a group of sixteen high-potential leaders within his corporation. As always, Stuart speaks with the unpretentious charm of the Midwestern boy next door. Stuart is the newly minted CEO of a multibillion-dollar global corporation that manufactures industrial products. He is an outspoken champion for aggressively leveraging synergies among his corporation's thirty-four individual operating companies. These individual companies are used to lots and lots of autonomy. Stuart's message of change, in short, is the equivalent of a cultural revolution.

His audience on that particular October afternoon hails from operating companies all around the world. Most have met Stuart before, but never in a setting this intimate. As Stuart elaborates on his vision for a more centralized corporate structure, Jeff, the quiet and well-spoken CFO of a company in Salt Lake City, dares a question:

"You know, Stuart, all of this takes a lot of extra time and effort, and it's been such a rotten year. We've had to let go of 30 percent of our workforce, and in any given week I don't feel like I have enough time to get even the most basic things done."

Jeff says it calmly and with respect, but it is one of those moments when you can hear the proverbial pin drop. Stuart thinks for a brief second and then approaches Jeff's table.

"Jeff, that is the one thing I struggle with every day. More than anything else. Since I became CEO six months ago, I simply never have enough time." Stuart pauses and collects his thoughts. "And I haven't figured this one out yet. I hope I will. It frustrates the heck out of me. But that's what it's like for me every week."

Of all the things Stuart could have said, this is a pretty darn flawless response. Honest. Vulnerable. Stuart shows his cracks. One can feel a collective sigh of relief the moment Stuart finishes his words. Whatever unspoken tension has been hovering in the air vanishes in an instant.

I do not use the word "authentic" to describe Stuart's response. "Authentic" and "vulnerable" are adjectives that are too often tossed about interchangeably these days. "Authentic" simply means that I show up fully aligned with my deepest beliefs and values, that I am conscious of these beliefs and values, and that I act in accordance with them. For the remainder of this book, I will assume that you and I both aspire to this level of alignment. If you do not—please stop reading now. This is not the book for you.

Here's where behavior really gets interesting for me. I can be authentic in so many different ways. I can be authentic when I laugh. When I'm pensive. When I'm silly. When I'm provocative. When I'm silent. When I'm vulnerable. Within the vast arena of potentially authentic behavior, there are so many ways of "showing up." What intrigue me are the choices you and I make. In that quick moment before Stuart answered Jeff's question, he made two millisecond decisions. Choice #1: Stuart elected to be vulnerable. And Choice #2: Stuart chose just "how" to be vulnerable.

Vulnerability involves taking a risk, it always does; authenticity may or may not. My vulnerability may mean that you may like me less because I don't have the answer you seek. You may like me less because I am not the idealized person you desire. You may like me less because I choose not to play nice. You may like me less because I reveal the very flaws you seek to hide within yourself.

The risk is real. But because we see another person take a risk, the potential reward for the risk-taker is tremendous. Stuart's response to his group revealed that he didn't have all of the answers (big risk for a CEO). And it created the additional benefit of unexpected common ground (remember our Belief #1!). Real, meaningful common ground.

Showing my cracks does not mean I tell you everything. It doesn't mean I over-share. It certainly doesn't mean I share indiscriminately. Folks who tell too much are simply folks who tell too much. We don't get to know them better because they tell us everything. No, we merely get to witness their oversized need to be heard. And then we tend to lose interest, fast. Really, really fast.

During a workshop I was co-leading with my friend Jennifer, she shared a male castration fantasy with our participants. I don't remember what audience comment compelled Jennifer to "go there," but I know I was startled. Why the heck did Jennifer talk about "that?" Was this an authentic comment? Sure. Vulnerable? Yes. Helpful? Well, what do you think? Jennifer's anecdote prompted a sudden embarrassed silence in the room. The not-so-good pin-drop kind of silence. A you-can-feel-them-cringe kind of moment.

During a three-day leadership retreat for emerging business leaders, Terrence, a senior director who had been bypassed for a VP position, talked at great length about his professional frustrations and his deeply ingrained belief that this company didn't value him. He talked about it a lot—during the conference, during the evening functions, over coffee breaks. Was he vulnerable? Sure. Terrence's chatter may have been a desperate cry for help, but it was the wrong place, wrong time for that conversation. It was, in fact, career suicide. A week later he was unceremoniously released from his suffering; his superiors sent him packing.

Helpful vulnerability means I have a sense of occasion. I have a hunch of what I may wish to reveal, in that moment, and I have an even clearer hunch that my revelation will advance the conversation, not impede it. I follow this hunch—and I pay attention to the impact my comments have on those around me.

Reality: The more successful I am in life, the greater the risk in the vulnerable moment. If I screw it up, I can screw up a lot of things, big time. But every time I show up with my social blinds drawn tight, I perpetuate a relationship that keeps out the light. Not taking any risks in showing the personal cracks guarantees that I will be viewed as a business robot that nobody really wants to work with.

BELIEF #4: DON'T GET STUCK WITH A LOSER.

It's the old joke about LA. You know, everyone you talk with is busy glancing over your shoulder, trying to spot someone else who is more important and whom they would rather speak with.

When they finally meet that someone else, he is busy glancing over their shoulder, of course! And so it goes . . .

I have been guilty of this behavior, just once or twice. (Gulp.) It can kick in when I attend an event with a sense of obligation and no actual desire to be there. And it can get me into real trouble at a function where I have a predetermined social goal. The sort of event where I am so darn sure of which person I absolutely "must" meet that evening. Suddenly everyone who is not my predetermined goal becomes a social barrier. And before I realize it, I'm tearing through one barrier after the next.

A loser? That might be anyone who cannot do anything for me, anyone who isn't attractive enough for me to be seen with, anyone who I deem to be socially inferior to me, anyone who is not exceptional in any immediately apparent way, anyone who is a little too quiet, anyone who is so different from me that he makes me uncomfortable. Anyone who is not "enough." And if my standards of enough-ness are extravagant, that could be a lot of people.

Does this sound just a little shallow to you? You bet. I also know that I have had such thoughts. Most of us have, at one point or another. For some of us, it is part of the unrelenting, daily people-editing we do every time we chat with absolutely anyone.

Some pretty self-important notions hide behind this first-impression-scanning:

Notion #1: My time is precious. It is so precious that I can really only focus on chatting with folks who meet my notion of whom I should be talking to. And that would be anybody but a loser . . .

Notion #2: I know what you have to tell me before you tell me. I've done my first-impression-scan, so I have an instant idea of who you are. I have been around, and I "know" people. Even if you say something that I might consider interesting if it were uttered by someone else, I won't really hear it when you say it, because my mind is already made up about who you are. Sorry.

Notion #3: I resent the fact that I got stuck talking to you. I will engage with you in a round or two of fake chatter because I do have good manners. I know how to play nice. But I will make sure that you feel how much, deep down, I really, really don't wish to speak with you.

Notion #4: I know whom I should be talking to. I do, I truly do—and believe me, you're not it.

This ceaseless split-second brain chatter supports another deeply ingrained notion about how to best engage with someone when there are quite a few other folks about. Think party, reception, networking event.

Notion #5: Circulate, circulate. If I stay too long chatting with one person, I will miss out on the opportunity to chat with someone else. That someone else, I am sure, will be a heck of a lot more interesting than the person I am talking to right now. I've learned this one boring conversation at a time. More is better.

Mind you, extricating ourselves with grace from a conversation we really do not wish to have is an essential social skill. Moving on is preferable to staying in a conversation where the other person is subjected to our shifty energy, our pressured sense of time, our robotic responses. Chances are, if we more often than not find ourselves in such conversations, we are either in the wrong job or hanging out in the wrong places. Or, much more likely, we are highly evolved devotees of our Belief #4—the anti-loser belief. Our sense of self-importance prevents the possibility of the sweet revelations that another person can offer us. We brashly sweep past moment after moment in which we might actually make a surprising connection. We are, thought by thought, killing the very thing we claim to desire.

Reality: It is far more powerful to connect with one person or just a few than to perpetually roam a room. When I am busy scheming for a conversation other than the one I'm in, I'm never in any conversation at all. I don't really want to be there, thus I'm not really there. So—if you don't wish to be there, please stay home. And if you are there, please decide to show up.

BELIEF #5: I WILL, I WILL, I WILL BE PERFECT

Once in a blue moon I get a "we don't know what's wrong" phone call. Allow me to describe. Mitch, a principal in a well-heeled accounting firm in New England, is frequently asked to speak at industry events, community gatherings, networking socials. His mentor Andrea calls me and tells me that, in those situations, Mitch often feels inarticulate. He struggles with finding the right words when he has to speak. Nobody is really quite sure of what sort of coaching might help Mitch. Does he need to improve his executive presence? Does he need a more expansive business vocabulary? Or is it simply a lack of confidence in high-stakes social settings?

When I meet Mitch I am struck by how likeable he is. I experience Mitch as smart, funny, poised, knowledgeable, engaging.

And, you bet, highly articulate. I notice the moments when Mitch pauses to search for the right next word. Yes, Mitch looks vulnerable in those moments. But while Mitch views such moments as a deficit, I experience them as a major asset. The moments are quick, though in Mitch's mind they seem to last forever. They do not undermine his credibility one bit. On the contrary, they help me to experience him as genuine and not slick. They make me appreciate the care with which Mitch crafts his message. They allow me to—literally and metaphorically—take a breath with him. And this breath brings me closer to Mitch.

Clearly "we don't know what's wrong with Mitch" because there's nothing wrong with Mitch! Mitch simply judges himself too harshly. More importantly, Mitch judges himself by some uberstandard for the perfect communication, the perfect public self. Does Mitch have things to work on? Sure. But the thing he's worried about the most—this notion that he is not meeting some unwritten standard of perfect public conduct—we toss out the window, at once.

We all have a little bit of Mitch in us. While Mitch is simply trying to figure out how to match a standard of being "on," a true perfectionist seeks to exceed this standard. He is "over-on." He smiles, and we see a tense eagerness in the smile. His muscles are taut, and we see the tight edge in every movement. He will not tolerate silence. He will interrupt you with the perfect verbal response while you speak. His verbal prowess will feel like an assault as he battles to not lose control of the conversation. You can't relax because he can't relax. You flinch. If he is a superior at work you suck it up and try to watch your back. If he isn't, you simply bolt. You certainly don't connect with him, ever.

I have many ways of describing to others what I do. When I feel mischievous I have been known to say that "I help to polish people with power." I say it with a twinkle in the eye and mental quotation marks, but as I jot down these words I recoil. I don't care for the word "polish." I don't care for the public behavior that it describes. Come to think of it, I don't like my glib little phrase at all!

Social polish is the outer manifestation of perfectionism. These two are evil identical twins. Yes, sometimes I meet folks whose public demeanor comes across as rough around the edges, and yes, they indeed benefit from a bit of un-roughing. Their roughness, whether it lies in the language they use or the etiquette they breach, inhibits the social connections they desire. Removing "rough" barriers is relatively easy. Un-polishing the over-polished individual is a whole other can of worms. (More about the social roles we choose to play in chapter 5.) The social role and the person beneath it are often entirely merged in the polished individual. A lifelong effort has gone into cultivating her polished mask. Scratch the polish, and she has little idea of how to behave. She breathes "polish." She speaks "polish." Her entire body acts "polish." A connection that transcends social platitudes becomes near impossible. Undoing the polish happens only with sincere and sustained determination. It requires showing the person beneath the role—-and that is likely someone the over-polished person doesn't know.

I am confident that you and I have our own personal notions of what a moment of great connection feels like. Many of us strive hard to make such a moment happen. It is, indeed, wonderful to have a vision for such a moment. If we can envision it, we are a heck of a lot more likely to allow it to happen. I use the word "allow" with keen intent. A perfectionist will try to force the moment. Truth is, I cannot "work at" a moment of connection. I cannot will it into existence. The more I try to force it, the more I block it. The beauty of a moment of connection is that it is not perfect. It does not need to be perfect. It transcends our limited notions of what perfection is. It is another one of those wonderful mysteries of life—the less I try to control it, the more likely it is to occur.

I am struck by a comment Judith Jamison made in an interview in the *New York Times*. One of the all-time great American dancers, Ms. Jamison was for years the leading female principal dancer with Alvin Ailey American Dance Theater. Since Alvin Ailey died, over twenty years ago now, Ms. Jamison has served as the company's artistic director. Dance is an art form in which performers worship perfection. In their quest for perfection, dancers train, train, and over-train. They injure themselves. They strive for a standard of greatness that even legendary dancers attain in fleeting moments only. (*Black Swan*, anyone?) Yet, in a recent interview about lessons she has learned about leadership, Jamison speaks not of perfection. No, she celebrates the opposite of it:

> One thing I cannot stand is when people say 'Hi, how are you?' and they don't wait to hear how I am. They're just going through the motions. I say to people: 'Keep it human. Keep it alive. Don't turn into a robot.' You have to hear what the other person is saying clearly. You have to listen, and really care, because we're all the same under the skin."[4]

Judith Jamison is right. An infectious connection begins in such little moments. Those are the moments that "keep it alive." An infectious connection trusts that each such moment will lead to another little moment and another one. And it celebrates the imperfection of every such moment.

Reality: *While striving for a perfect meeting, a perfect conversation, a perfect party, a perfect relationship is noble, most social scientists will tell us that such things don't exist. The notion of perfection negates the wonders of all that is not perfect—the beauty of the awkward moment, the thrill of the unrehearsed encounter, the surprise of the delicious social detour. Perfection is based on an idealized definition of a social connection. It is like holding on to a scene from a perfect Hollywood movie that we have never experienced in our own lives but attempt to recreate on a daily basis.*

SUMMARY

Most of us yearn for connection. And even if this isn't the deepest of our yearnings, we understand that being able to connect is vital to our success in the world. In our quest to connect, we are guided by a wealth of beliefs about how to best go about doing just that. Some of these beliefs may be very conscious and clearly articulated in our minds. Most of them likely are not.

Here are the five most persistent beliefs that block a genuine connection. Guaranteed.

1. Find common ground—fast

Common ground is delicious when it is earned. Common ground is irrelevant when it is forced. Take your time to discover common ground—and relish the many things that you do not have in common.

2. Avoid charged topics

This belief banishes us to a swirl of unending breezy social banter. Such banter helps to kill time and fosters the illusion of connection—a connection that has little meaning and less value.

3. Don't show the cracks

My vulnerable moment allows the other person to relax around me and take her own personal risks. But every time I show up with my social blinds drawn tight, I perpetuate a relationship that keeps out the light. Not taking any risks in showing the personal cracks guarantees that I will be viewed as a business robot that nobody really wants to play with.

4. Don't get stuck with a loser

When I am busy scheming for a conversation other than the one I'm in, I'm never in any conversation at all. The person I am speaking with becomes the social barrier I must overcome. Since I don't really want to be there,

I'm not really there. So please, if you are there, decide to show up.

5. I will, I will, I will be perfect

The notion of perfection negates the wonders of all that is not perfect—the beauty of the awkward moment, the thrill of the unrehearsed encounter, the surprise of the delicious social detour. Perfection is based on an idealized definition of a social connection, a definition already dwarfed by our attempt to quantify the unquantifiable.

The need to do it perfectly is the ultimate barrier, the mother of all connection roadblocks. It rolls the four previous beliefs into one tight little recipe for disaster. This recipe creates one stunted connection after another and, worse yet, puts us into the prison of fake conversations. It lock us up, with little chance of parole.

Stay out of jail, please. In the upcoming chapters, as we dive deeper into our 4 Levels of Connection, you will find many practical tools that will help you to do just that. So, let's begin!

Chapter 2

Level One: Language Is an Aphrodisiac

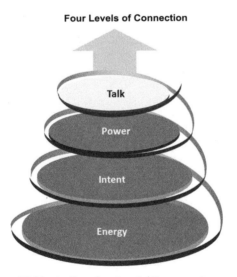

Table 2: Our first level of connection

When I was an undergraduate theater major, I was required to take dance classes. Modern technique, jazz. Well, I loathed those classes. If you have ever been to a dance class, you know how it goes. The instructor demonstrates a combination of steps. Dancers then travel in small groups across the dance floor, repeating the combination. The experienced groups tend to go first. The midlevel groups follow, and then the groups that just can't keep up limp across toward the end.

You can guess which part of the pack I was in, right? Following a series of dance steps I had not chosen, attempting to meet a standard set by the very skilled instructor—this all seemed completely alien to me. It felt like an utterly unenjoyable way of moving through space. It was as if I was trying to learn a language I did not wish to speak.

Now, the moment I discovered movement improvisation, I was happy. A group of performers move through space at the same time, sometimes to music, often not. They do not mimic a previously taught combination. As they move, their movement choices are informed by what they are sensing, in that moment, within them and around them. It is informed by the movements of their fellow dancers. They can approach each other, partner for a while, leave. Themes emerge as movements repeat themselves. Now, this was a language I DID want to learn!

Every conversation is a little like a movement improvisation, isn't it? Unless we're queued up in a receiving line to meet Queen Elizabeth, there is no combination of tidy dance steps we follow. Each conversation is a dance that we discover as it unfolds, with its own rhythm, flavor, flow. The pleasure we and our partners derive from this dance will depend in no small measure on how well we improvise, moment by moment, phrase by phrase, instinct by instinct.

And yes—on how well we talk!

It's been drilled into me that listening is more important than talking, but all thoughts bring me back to this: At some point in a conversation, I have to say something. What I say will influence the flow of the conversation. I sure hope what I say demonstrates that I have heard you. More importantly, I hope that you will be engaged by my talk, and that my talk inspires your talk. If my talk improvises well with your talk—watch out, we're going to have one hell of a time!

If you are a bilingual or multilingual person, you have learned about the power of language the hard way. Chances are, one of the languages you speak is more dominant than the other. German is my mother tongue, but English is the language I speak daily now. It is the language in which I write and the language in which I dream. It is the language in which I babble freely, without ever second-guessing myself. My German is fluent, but my German conversations are fraught with moments of hesitation. I search for a word, I stumble in midsentence. My German chats don't flow as well as my English-language ones. I feel impaired in my ability to connect, and that's not a good feeling at all!

When I was training New York City teenagers to become mediators, nearly every skill revolved around the crisp use of language. Mediation language is grown-up stuff. Mediators validate, paraphrase, reflect feelings, identify issues. These skills come with a set of suggested verbiage that sounds unfamiliar to even the most illumined adult. During our three-day training programs, it was clear that my teenagers couldn't say this language "the textbook way." It would make them sound like fake wannabe-adults. Well, we encouraged them to take the principles of each communication tool and discover their own way of saying the words. The results were astounding! What I learned from my students, big time, is just how much language can empower us. And I am not referring to the use of highfalutin language. No, we are empowered because we know how to use language both strategically and instinctively, and we know how to do it with finesse.

My teenagers simply couldn't stop talking.

I hope the five principles in our Talk Level will have a similar impact on you. These principles are simple—very, very simple.

There are skills that support these principles. These skills are not so simple at all, but they are a language that is easily learned. Practice these principles, and you will do the conversation improvisation dance with a sense of mastery. As you practice them every day, you will no longer need to consciously evoke them. They will simply be part and parcel of how you "show up." Your mastery will be invisible to others, but your ease and confidence will not!

PRINCIPLE #1: INVITE ME IN

Have you noticed? More and more of us speak in person as if we're sending an email. I find myself listening to sound bites instead of developed ideas. I hear bullet points instead of sentences. Stop, please. Entice me. Seduce me. Invite me in.

I use the phrase "invitational language" when I coach an executive on how to speak in high-stakes settings. Most presentations I observe tend to start with what I call "procedural language." Crisp, efficient, spare, with little personal color added. "Hi. I'm Joe Pasternak, and I'm here to talk about operational excellence. This is my agenda . . ."

Really, Joe? And you expect me to care?

Let's dwell on this formal context for a moment, because the same principle applies to any setting in which we speak, formal or not. In a formal setting, I look for language cues that entice me. Phrases such as "I'm happy to speak with you today," or "I have been looking forward to spending this hour with you," or "I'm thrilled that you all showed up today." Basic welcoming words. I offer you examples of language that I like and that, depending on the circumstance, I may use. It is language that feels sincere to me when I say it—provided, of course, that it matches my sentiment about the social situation I find myself in, or the individual I am speaking with. Please do not use my language; I urge you to find your own words. And please, please stay away from the well-trodden cliché. "Thank you for taking time out of your busy day" is not a welcome—it's a condescending platitude.

Anthony Robbins, the quintessential self-reinvention guru, says it beautifully. "People with impoverished vocabularies live emotionally impoverished lives. People with rich vocabularies have a multihued palette of colors with which to paint their life's experience, not only for others, but for themselves, as well."[5]

Invitational language is a crucial part of this palette, and emotional cue words are the core ingredient of invitational language. Good old-fashioned adjectives, the kind of words that we have banished from most written communication these days. Now, you may view yourself as a logical rather than an emotional person. You may believe that you don't "click" with this sort of emotive language. You may be quite certain of this because you know how your brain works.

Guess what—Madison Avenue knows better. It understands that a commitment to any sort of message is ultimately based on emotion. Pretty much all advertisement, serious or lighthearted, gets our attention with images and emotional cues that resonate deeply with our core desires, dreams, and aspirations. Yes, the marketing folks got it right. Emotional signals work. Research consistently shows that even the most logical person is ultimately seduced by an emotional message. It's a little bit like flattery. You may frown upon your colleague Jim, who's always complimenting folks. Guess what again—Jim is no fool. Even when the compliment is a little cheesy or way too obvious, even when a comment doesn't seem to entirely match reality, it still works. Flattery makes us feel good. And even the most logical individual likes that!

1. Types of emotional cueing

How does emotional cueing show up in everyday language? There are two types of phrases that draw my conversation partner deeper into a conversation: Phrases that I offer to get a conversation rolling, and phrases that I say in response to a comment made by the other person. The sample phrases below are intended as guidance and inspiration. Use them if they match your current speaking style. If they don't, tweak them, or find words of your own.

Phrases that I offer (an invitation that draws the other person in):

- *I have so looked forward to . . .*
- *I am eager to find out . . .*
- *I can't wait to discuss . . .*
- *I am curious about . . .*
- *I am thrilled that . . .*
- *I would love to better understand . . .*
- *I so want to learn more about . . .*

Phrases that I say in response (an invitation to a deeper conversation):

- *I got a kick out of what you just said.*
- *I never thought of it this way before.*
- *I was surprised by . . .*
- *Your comments help me better understand . . .*
- *You made me look at this in a whole new way . . .*
- *I was tickled by . . .*
- *Your thoughts got me right in my gut . . .*

This is basic feel-good language that evokes positive emotions in the speaker as well as in the listener. Do you read such phrases and think to yourself: "I'm not comfortable using that kind of language! I would never say that! That just isn't me!"

Let's flip this line of thinking, shall we? How about "I'm not fully comfortable using such language—yet!" Be uncomfortable and say your lines anyway. Discomfort just means I'm tapping into something that's outside of my zone of habitual behavior. My habitual zone of behavior is, by definition, a limited zone. Think of appropriating emotional cue words as learning a foreign language. It may not feel comfortable at first. It may, in fact, feel quite uncomfortable for a pretty long time. It will take practice—lots of practice. But eventually, as you persist, you will cross the threshold when it suddenly feels like you have always spoken this language. The words just tumble out of your mouth, with no deliberate effort on your part. Sweet.

2. Expanding our vocabulary

This is how I explore language with a client. Take Melissa. She is the Regional Sales Director for a national sales force. Much of the communication Melissa has with her team takes place during conference calls. Feedback revealed that many folks on her team felt that Melissa wasn't sufficiently engaging them during these calls. As we reviewed some of this feedback together, Melissa observed that she doesn't really know how to make appreciative comments: "I realize that all I ever say is 'That's great . . . !'"

Melissa's assignment? Find ten other ways of saying "that's great" and write them down. Sounds simple, doesn't it? Ten phrases is actually a whole lot of language. Melissa came up with eight. But once Melissa started using these eight phrases in her calls, she felt a new sense of confidence in responding to the many comments folks made during these calls. Responding became a lot more fun. And this sense of fun was felt by others, immediately!

3. Your vocabulary expansion exercise

Here's an assignment. It will take no more than fifteen to twenty minutes to complete, and it will change the tone of every conversation you have.

- Write down ten phrases you can say to invite another person into a conversation.
- Write down ten phrases you can say to respond to a comment that has stimulated you.
- Start to play with these phrases in conversations.
- Enjoy!

PRINCIPLE #2: OPEN THE DOORS

In 1990, I left my life as a theater director in Manhattan and moved to the small island of Tobago. I left to become a windsurfer.

25

I left because I had a recurring vision of living in a white house on a tropical island. I left without any deep purpose; I went to Tobago to just hang out and "be." The purpose of my life on this island became clear to me only after my final return to New York.

I'm merely giving you the headlines here, but I trust this much is clear: There are a lot of stories in Tobago. They are juicy and fun. They describe a year that changed my life. If you dig into this conversation, you'll find out a thing or two about me.

I don't actually have a great yearning to talk about Tobago—this all occurred over twenty years ago, after all. However, when a conversation steers into themes and experiences that make me think of my life in Tobago, I'll put out a cue. I won't tell you the entire story right away, ever. But I'll give you a cue like "in the early '90s I spent a year living on the small island of Tobago." Simple, right?

1. Every cue is a door.

When someone throws out a cue that is unexpected or surprising—notice it.

Imagine a long hallway that seems to go on forever. Each side of the hallway is lined with one door after another, and each door is closed. The hallway shimmers in a brilliant white light. White is the color of nothing and everything; it is the color of memory and the color of possibility. Each conversation is a stroll down this long white hallway, and each cue we hear is an invitation to open one of the doors.

When I offer a Tobago cue, 90 percent of the time I receive a response like "Oh, that's really cool." It is usually quite heartfelt. And then we flit on to another topic.

I chuckle as I read an interview in *Vanity Fair*. The great film director Mike Nichols and the actress Julia Roberts are speaking with *Vanity Fair* about, among other things, the art of the conversation. In this excerpt they refer to their respective spouses, Diane Sawyer and Danny Moder.

Julia Roberts: The manners that I was brought up with—and this doesn't work well when doing press at a young age—is when someone asks you a question, you answer it. Then you wait to be asked another question. It's not very conversational; it doesn't show a great deal of interest in the other person. You're kind of cutting yourself off from a whole world of other people's opinions. Diane and Danny both have that art of true interest in other people, other situations, other ideas. I've learned about that artfulness from both of them.

Mike Nichols: One of the things that fascinates me about Diane, who goes all over the world all the time—she's in Afghanistan, she's in Iraq, she's everywhere and then back in a day and a half—is that no one ever asks her about what she saw.

Julia Roberts: But Diane has the most interesting stuff to tell you about anything!

Mike Nichols: People, by and large, would rather be talking than listening.[6]

I am struck by Mr. Nichols' observation that no one asks Diane Sawyer a question. This lack of interrogatives may be prompted by our sense of Ms. Sawyer's professional role. After all, she is the one who asks the questions, right? But, please—if you are speaking with Ms. Sawyer, open the door! "The art of true interest" is a delicious phrase. We are isolating the ingredients of this art right here, right now.

2. Walk through the door.

We walk through the door by asking curiosity questions. *What did you like about living in Tobago? How did you spend your time in Tobago?* "What" and "how" questions invite clarification. They yield details. "What" and "how" questions are easy questions that are not intrusive. The other person remains fully in charge of just what he reveals.

Better yet are the "why" questions. *Why did you move to Tobago?* "Why" questions show my conversation partner that I am interested in what makes her tick. I'm not just curious about the events in her life, I'm interested in her motivations, aspirations, dreams, desires. Very cool.

And please refrain from the "when" and "where" questions. *When did you move to Tobago? Where in Tobago did you live?* You may be eager to know some of these details, but chances are, if that information is crucial to the conversation that's unfolding, your partner will tell you, anyway. Ask a few of these questions in a row, and the rhythm of the conversation stagnates. We suddenly become the interrogator who is hunting for clues, the detective who's grilling the suspect. Not cool at all!

3. Do NOT fake the curiosity.

Not every cue will beckon you. Fine. Not every door needs to be opened. Maybe Tobago life is not something you wish to hear about. Maybe Isabel tells you that she has a long-standing drinking problem, and you think to yourself—gee, I don't know if I want to walk down that path right now. Good—don't walk down that path. Key is that you heard the cue, and that you made a deliberate choice to not open this door.

4. Sometimes, DO fake the curiosity.

Allow me to explain. I am often surrounded by folks who love to play golf. It seems to be the sport-de-rigueur in many of the circles in which I travel. No matter how hard I try, nothing in me is interested in golf. I don't yearn to watch it, don't yearn to play it. This sport simply does not get my juices flowing!

Now, I don't inject fake golf-enthusiasm into a conversation. But I am always interested in finding out what makes my conversation partner tick. Think of Julia Roberts and the art of curiosity. Switch the conversation from the surface chatter (golf) to a below-the-surface inquiry (motivation for golf). That's a door I will happily open, with anyone! Here's where I fall back on a "what" or "why" question. Suddenly the conversation shifts from talking about the mechanics of playing golf or the explication of recent golf scores to a deeper understanding of what provides joy to my conversation partner. And that always makes for a scrumptious chat.

5. The present is a brilliant door.

There are times when a conversation just doesn't seem to click. My conversation partner and I are not picking up on each other's cues. There's door after door that I do not wish to open. Well, I can certainly opt out and find a more palatable conversation partner. If social circumstances do not permit such an exit, I can always choose to converse about the present.

Look around. Notice what's happening in your surroundings. See the elderly couple that's holding hands, sitting on the boardwalk bench just behind you (I live in South Florida, so this is a Florida snapshot). Notice the sun that is just starting to peek through a batch of clouds. Watch the young lady whose parasail is looping into the sky. Hear the two little boys who screech with joy as they fling their torsos into a wave. Catch the din of Russian and French chatter as clusters of people parade past you.

Remember false common ground? Whatever is happening in the moment, around us, is real common ground. We are both witnessing the same event, but each of us quite likely fixates on a different detail, views it through our own particular lens. Our stories about what we see are usually not the same, at all. Now, that can be really interesting!

There's a prerequisite, of course, to having a chat about the present. We have to actually be "present." We have to be fully in the physical moment, mind and spirit, to notice what's going on around us. When we habitually jabber on our smartphones while we order a mocha latte or check email messages as we zoom down the freeway, much of the present moment will zoom right past us, as well.

6. Take a risk.

Here's a recent business dinner conversation that left me wanting for more. We talked about sex.

Sanjeev is the chatty VP of Sales for a global high-tech firm. During the six months or so in which I have known him, his communication style has been consistently safe, mainstream, in-the-box. Pleasant but unsurprising.

Well, this evening Sanjeev mentions that his 12-year-old son is coming to him with questions about procreation. Sanjeev explains that in his native India, he had never had that sort of conversation with his dad. These questions by his son make him just a bit uncomfortable, and he's not sure how to respond.

Is Sanjeev taking a risk? You bet, and a wonderful one. We know that family life is not always simple or smooth. Statistics show that just under 50 percent of U.S. marriages end up in divorce. Yet in business, folks still tell the happy-fairytale-family-story over and over with great pep, without diving into any of the complexities of their family lives.

Sanjeev's musings prompt many opinions at our table. Cindy Reynolds, the VP of Human Resources, tells of the moment when her sixteen-year-old daughter came to her to talk about sex. Cindy recounts with great relish that this was the moment she, the mom, had been both dreading and looking forward to, all at the same time. Finally, she was having the mother–daughter conversation about sexuality! Well, it turned out to be the conversation in which her daughter announced that she had already been having intercourse with her boyfriend—for a good three months!

Is Cindy taking a risk here? You bet. We're definitely no longer having the my-perfect-family with my-perfect-daughter story. We're in real life now.

As I listen to my dinner-mates I recall an evening that I spent with a client of mine, Dr. Sherry Armstrong-Wilkinson. I decide to tell the story. Sherry is a British physician with a salt-of-the-earth personality. She was attending a week-long training program I was leading in Midtown Manhattan. In chat after chat Sherry carried on about how much she loathed Manhattan. Well, I did something I normally would not do in the midst of a training week: I invited Sherry out to a meal in the West Village, the neighborhood where I lived at the time. I was determined to show her a Manhattan she would love. Little did I know!

Over dinner, Sherry confided in me that she moonlighted as a sex therapist and had a penchant for sex toys. When I mentioned that there were several sex shops on Christopher Street, right around the corner from us—off we went. We did not just go into one sex shop. We went into every sex shop on Christopher Street. I leave you with the image of me stroking a bunch of different-sized rubber penises to help Sherry decide which ones she wanted to buy.

A risk? Sherry took one by confiding in me about her sex therapist work. Did I take one, as well, by telling the story? It didn't feel like a big one—but truth is, we don't often talk about going to a sex shop at a formal event, in mixed company.

This was not an evening of drunken confessions at the bar that you regret the morning after. It was simply a case of a group of folks noticing the doors and walking through them. At this table, for this particular meal, everyone tossed Beliefs #2 and #3 from the previous chapter out the window: We talked about charged topics. We revealed the cracks in our facades.

I didn't feel tired after this dinner. I felt stimulated by the honesty. Energized by the laughter. Buoyed by the conversation. I did not want it to end!

7. Be curious about the world.

When I was a young acting student at the Washington Theatre Lab, I yearned to acquire acting technique. I wanted to inhale the teachings of Jerzy Grotowski and Konstantin Stanislavsky, my two great idols. I was sure that if I soaked up every word of wisdom these gurus had to offer, I would, by osmosis, become a great actor.

Here's what Tony Abeson, my acting teacher, asked of me instead: "Become an interesting person. Be curious about the world. Go to a museum. Meditate on nature. Read, read, read."

Tony's advice infuriated me. I wanted a method of acting, not a sermon! I appreciate Tony's wisdom a good deal more with the passing of time, and I wholeheartedly second his sentiments. I have close friends who pride themselves on not owning a television set. I have colleagues who defiantly announce they don't read newspapers. I have spiritual comrades who decry the Internet as a major source of distraction that interferes with inner peace.

I "get" this desire to shield ourselves from the media version of reality. I write these words a couple of days after Whitney Houston was found dead. My first impulse: Let me run from the tsunami of Whitney media overkill. I had never been much of a Whitney Houston fan, anyway! Truth is, however, as someone who daily chats with people from many different walks of life, it behooves me to keep abreast of current events. "Well, I never watch television, it's full of junk and a waste of time," means I give up on the cultural framework within which I do my social dance.

Yes, I ended up watching Jennifer Hudson's tribute to Whitney Houston at the Grammy Awards. Her rendition of "I Will Always Love You" sent shivers down my spine. The human voice—how stirring, how beautiful it is! Piers Morgan devoted his entire next program on CNN to Whitney Houston. He interviewed Chaka Khan. Should I watch? Should I work on my book? Well, as I listened to the interview with Chaka Khan, I was deeply touched by Ms. Khan's articulate and vulnerable reflections on her own tussles with drug addiction.

I don't regret a second I spent on these diversions. And the next morning, as I sat at the counter of the JP Bagels coffee shop in Hollywood, munching on my two poached eggs and onion bagel, I contributed with pleasure to the Whitney chitchat. Yum.

PRINCIPLE #3: HAVE A POINT OF VIEW

As my friend Raul Rodriguez and I file out of the theater after a performance of the play *The Motherf***er with the Hat,* I overhear a woman behind us asking her friend: "So what did you think of the play?"

The friend answers: "I need to go home and think about it."

Excuse me? You just attended a play that elicited gales of laughter from the audience, that featured the "f" word in every other line of dialogue, a play that provocatively dove into the world of addiction and recovery and personal betrayal—and you have no opinion?

Are you kidding me?

I enjoyed this play and its very visceral production at Miami's Gables Stage. That's my point of view. I can give you lots of explanations of what exactly I loved about this play, but that will have to wait for a private conversation. I can just as easily see why another person might not like this play at all. OK—so tell me. Please have your perspective. And let's talk.

The notion of having a clear point of view seems to have gotten a bad rap in recent years. We celebrate ambiguity. We confuse having a point of view or opinion with claiming to be right. We associate being right with the demands of the ego, our false self who needs to wield control over any social situation. We condemn opinions as a form of mental attachment to the illusory physical world we inhabit. Because, after all is said and done, we know there is a larger spiritual realm that transcends our fixation on the physical world. Right? And in this larger realm, our silly viewpoints simply don't matter. They are just another form of attachment to all that is not real . . .

The preceding narrative has a point of view. I believe in the gist of that narrative (another viewpoint). But in the meantime, while we're down here on earth together, let us not be afraid to have our own perspectives and state them. Let us not pretend to be more enlightened than we are. All of us have a point of view about lots and lots of things. Pretending we don't is a supremely unenlightened act. It's also a big fat lie.

Why should you and I bother telling our points of view? Your perspective tells me about yourself. What you find interesting, what you don't find interesting. What you value, what motivates you. Folks with a clear perspective tend to be a good deal more compelling than folks without one. Your viewpoint advances our conversation. It invites my viewpoint. If you're going to talk with me for any substantial amount of time, please have a strong perspective about something now and then!

Here are some tips to consider as we articulate our points of view:

1. Language matters.
Example #1: *New York City is a very noisy and fast-paced city.* You may agree with this statement. It is stated like a fact, but it is really just an opinion. When we consistently state opinions as facts, we invite instant rebuttals.

Example #2: *I find New York to be a very noisy and fast-paced city.* It is clearly stated as an opinion now, not as a fact. An opinion tends to be stated in a brief sentence or two.

A point of view is a more considered perspective that offers examples, experiences, and facts to substantiate our point of view. It's an opinion backed up with a bit of evidence:

Example #3: *I find New York City to be a very noisy and fast-paced city. When I stay in my hotel on Forty-First Street I have to keep windows shut all night, otherwise the street noise will keep me awake. When I walk down any street in midtown I find myself walking way faster than I normally do. I feel like I get swept along by the tide.* Our statement has now become a substantiated point of view. An opinion is easily dismissed. Because a viewpoint is more carefully considered, it demands a more substantive response, and the conversation deepens!

2. Phrases that signal a point of view

The following phrases clearly indicate to your listener that you're about to state a viewpoint.

- *I feel strongly that . . .*
- *I believe firmly in . . .*
- *I have always thought it was important to . . .*
- *I prefer to . . .*
- *I suggest that we . . .*
- *I have learned from past experience that . . .*

3. Let the other person off the hook.

"Schlagfertigkeit" is a German word that describes a person's ability to quickly retort and rebut a point someone else has made. It is viewed as a highly desirable skill in Germany. It implies that I am "good with words." I can outdo, outsmart anyone in any conversation. I am quick on my feet, and I know how to have the final word whenever I choose.

Sounds good, right? Such verbal agility is helpful if both parties enjoy a fast game of mental ping-pong. In all other situations, *Schlagfertigkeit* does little to foster a deeper sense of connection. It will, instead, create an "I'm right, you're wrong" or an "I will always be smarter than you" dynamic with the other person. While that may satisfy your competitive instincts, it may also stop your conversation dead in its tracks.

Smart conversationalists encourage a divergent perspective. They "own" their viewpoints and are, at the same time, comfortable hearing another person's perspective. MSNBC's early morning talk-fest, *Morning Joe*, is a rare media model for how a bunch of smart folks can sit around a table and actively toss divergent thoughts into the mix without instantly negating the other person. *Morning Joe* demonstrates a conversational culture in which conversationalists, more often than not, choose to let each other off the hook!

4. Phrases that elicit a point of view

If fresh viewpoints do not readily come forth in a conversation, try some of the following cues to elicit them. Remember—by inviting a divergent point of view, I encourage a complex and potentially more satisfying conversation.

- *You may see this very differently. I would love to know . . .*
- *What is another perspective that may be helpful to consider?*
- *Your experience of this may be very different from mine . . .*
- *There has to be another way to look at this. What do you think?*
- *Please give me your unedited thoughts on what I just said . . .*

5. Know your personal platform.

The moment I move into a senior leadership role in an organization, I am expected to know what I stand for. More importantly, I am expected to know how to cleanly articulate it. Let's call this a personal platform. This platform usually includes a mix of visions and goals, priorities, personal values. A platform is a whole bunch of viewpoints rolled into one. As a leader at the C-level, I need to be able to talk about this platform in any setting, with preparation or without, at the drop of a dime.

Doesn't sound so tough, does it? Well, if I have spent much of my career taking orders and not having a point of view, or if every time I state a point of view I annoy the heck out of people because I don't let them off the hook—not so easy. Couple this with the fact that at the C-level, every word I utter will be scrutinized with a microscope—it just got tougher. Add the fact that a platform tends to resort to universal principles and ideas that can easily sound trite—wow, we have our work cut out here!

Mike O'Sheehan is the brand-new chief of a major New England law firm with twenty-five partners. Mike is sharp, quick-witted, bursting with ideas. The quintessential caged animal, ready to bust loose with a sudden quip or comment. Mike is taking the six months prior to becoming the new president to clarify his platform. He starts this process by embracing the firm's values, which he inherited: "Trust. Integrity. Professionalism." Blah blah blah blah blah blah blah. Pretty words, instantly trite. They hang on the wall of every other firm in downtown Boston. They don't distinguish or differentiate. Mike's three personal cornerstones for his platform: "Profitability. Accountability. Growth." More pretty words. Lots more blah blah blah blah blah blah blah.

How does Mike "un-trite" the clichés? How does he reappropriate language that the business world has been chewing on, chewing up, and spitting out for so long that it lacks any semblance of relevance? Mike does it by sticking to the basics we're exploring in this chapter. He begins to imbue his concepts with emotional cue words. He searches for language that will invite his constituents to discover these concepts anew. He rehearses conveying his very personal take on these words (his point of view). And he considers stories he can tell that will allow these words to fully resonate with new meaning. Which takes us right to Principle #4.

PRINCIPLE #4: OWN YOUR STORIES.

Stories just make sense. They provide a magical way of opening a door into our lives. They are a shining example of language that entices, of talk that takes a risk. Stories also take us back to a state of childlike delight in discovering the world. I think of lying under the billowing down comforters in my grandmother's heavy wooden bed, listening to her tell stories of how she grew up. Those moments were delicious. When Omi told stories I felt transported to a whole mysterious world of the past. A world I knew only through the stories she could tell. You may have your own memories of storytelling time in kindergarten, or you may think of rushing to the phone to tell your best friend about something thrilling that just happened that day. Your personal story.

Since I was four years old I have led a traveling life. I travel a lot now, and we traveled incessantly when I was a child. Here's something I learned during my traveling years. Differences aside, all cultures love food, and all cultures love stories. Let me say it even more emphatically: Folks all over the world share a hunger for great stories. Stories (and movies as our modern-day equivalent of old-school storytelling) are a primary way in which we make sense of the world and begin to understand each other.

Especially if the story is well told.

If you're fortunate, you're a natural storyteller. I think of the food-TV personality Paula Deen. John Leguizamo. Bill Clinton. Whoopi Goldberg. Kathy Griffin. Bill Cosby. David Sedaris. Chris Rock. Storytelling seems to be something these folks do with no effort at all. Quite a few of them are comics and craft their stories with great care. What do they have in common? They trust the details. They don't rush the delivery. The good news is, these skills can easily be learned.

THE STORIES WE TELL

There are three types of stories we tend to tell:

Moment Stories: I describe a moment that happened in my life. The details I tell will help you to connect with my experience of the moment, and they will likely help you to better understand me. My details, quite often, will also help you to connect with parts of yourself that you had forgotten. Remember Orhan Pamuk?

Meaning Stories: I describe a moment that happened in my life, and I offer my understanding of what that moment has meant to me or may mean to others. We rarely know the meaning of a moment when it first unfolds. Meaning is revealed with the passing of time, and with considerable reflection. Meaning Stories are mature stories. They are the gift of an examined life.

Life Stories: I describe a major chunk of my life and give it meaning. Key themes emerge as I reflect on a whole series of moments in my life, and I discover the thematic links between those moments. A Life Story is a bunch of meaning stories all rolled up into one. It offers a clear narrative about a major aspect of my life. Because I likely have more than one narrative about any aspect of my life, a Life Story is the narrative I choose to share with the rest of the world.

Here are two versions of a story from my life.

A MOMENT STORY

In April of 1967, when I was twelve years old, my parents, my brother Thomas and I went to visit the lost city of Petra in the south of Jordan. I had read in our Baedeker guidebook that Petra was called "the lost city" because it was forgotten for hundreds of years. The only way to enter Petra was through a long and very narrow canyon. The canyon was so narrow that during heavy rains, travelers had drowned as the water rose within the canyon.

We parked our Ford Taunus on a roadside near Petra and hired four camels and guides. As we left the road and rode down a slope into the desert, the entrance to the canyon appeared. The light inside the canyon was very murky and dark. The air quickly became cool. The canyon walls became so narrow that we were forced to ride single file. I could touch either side of the canyon with my hands, and I could no longer see the sky above the canyon.

And then it began to rain. The rain came down suddenly and very, very fast. Instantly every part of my body was drenched with water. My skin was quivering from the cool air and cold water. As I looked ahead I could no longer see the other camels. All I saw was a blurry gray wall of water rushing down from the sky. I called my parents' names but I could not hear my voice. I could not hear any answer. I heard nothing but the thundering roar of water coming down.

My guide yanked my camel down to the ground. I realized that he had pulled the camel and me into a cave. Water kept dripping from my body. The camel crouched low and heaved. My guide was flinging himself to the ground in rhythmic motions, praying in Arabic. The prayer sounded like an extended, mournful wail. The air inside the cave was chilly and damp. I looked out to the rain that was rushing down the entrance of the cave and pelting the ground. I saw nothing beyond this gray wall of rain. And for a moment I thought to myself, I don't know if I will ever see my parents or my brother again.

This story lives in the details. It invites you into an adventurous moment from my childhood. Truth is, my ride into Petra was not merely another adventurous escape from my childhood travels. It was an experience that left an indelible impression on me for the remainder of my life.

So here's the Meaning Story variant of my trip to Petra. Imagine that I have shared with you the same details I outlined above—and now I add the meaning perspective.

A MEANING STORY

That moment in the cave was the first time in my life that I felt a deep, deep terror. It was a brutal, gut-wrenching terror. It was as if I knew, without being able to put it into words, that everything could be taken away, in an instant. That there were forces in the world that were larger than my family and me, forces that we would never be able to control. I also knew, for the very first time in my life, that I deeply loved my parents.

It can be wonderful to tell a Moment Story without adding the perspective of the Meaning Story. By not offering my meaning, the listener is able to infer her own meaning. It allows for a truly personal connection to—and interpretation of—a story. Sometimes it is simply fun to tell a good story and tell it well, especially when we trust that the story will inherently be engaging for our listener.

A Meaning Story, however, elevates a conversation to a heightened insight into the moments that shape our lives. It offers a grown-up, sophisticated perspective on an event. More importantly, it encourages a similar level of thoughtfulness in our conversation partner. It nearly always invokes a new level of intimacy with another person.

LIFE STORIES

I remember sitting in a hotel bar in Midtown Manhattan, shooting the breeze with a group of fellow training professionals. Liz was the training director for one of the big blue-chip investment firms on Wall Street. She was the archetypal "tough broad"—earthy, wise, direct, with a giant heart of gold. As Liz chattered about her life she made the following observation: "I totally change my life every seven years. About six years ago I left Paris and moved to Manhattan. It's that time again. I feel another big change coming up."

It was a simple, off-the-cuff comment, but just then Liz's remark meant a lot to me. I had been a theater director for many years, had delivered some trainings in the not-for-profit world, but this was my first week of working as a corporate trainer. I had lots of doubts about whether this was the right path for me. Liz's perspective on her life story liberated me. It was a gift. I didn't need to know what the rest of my life would look like—this was just what I was doing in my life, right then.

The family story is one of our classic life stories. Every time we meet someone new, we eventually end up talking about family. Tina Governo is the VP of Organizational Development at Dover Corporation, an $8 billion Fortune 500 company. She is one of a handful of senior female leaders at Dover, and a highly visible female role model within the corporation. Tina talks freely about her daughter Emmy. At times she mentions simply that Emmy has a disability. At other times Tina will elaborate and explain that Emmy is quadriplegic and nonspeaking and requires 24/7 home care. Tina states this as one of the facts of her family story. She does not do so to elicit sympathy or to dominate the conversation. She does not linger on this information unless folks stop to inquire. And within her business culture, which tends to value a traditional family narrative, Tina talks just as freely about how she co-parents Emmy with her ex-husband, from whom she has long been divorced.

Tina "owns" her story. It's not a traditional, easy-breezy family story. Tina has made a deliberate choice to "tell" and doesn't edit out the messy pieces. It's a considered narrative. More importantly, Tina's ease in telling this story always brings folks closer to her!

Tina has reconciled some of the questions we all face when telling the family story. How do I tell my story when my family life is a bit untidy? When perchance I am not happily married? When I'm single and everyone around me is married? When I'm lesbian or gay and not "out" in my workplace? How do I tell it when my life choices have fallen well outside of what's considered the "norm?"

I have a brother who committed suicide in 1999. In the years right after his death I was unsure of how to answer the "Do you have siblings?" question. Sometimes I was simply not in the mood to disclose my brother's suicide; I was still sorting out my feelings about what had happened, and I didn't feel like having the "suicide conversation." Top it off with the fact that my brother committed suicide under rather gruesome circumstances, and I was truly at a loss. Should I share those details? If you asked me about siblings, I might have told you that I was an only child, or that I had a brother who had died. End of story.

I no longer claim to be an only child. That's too convenient a lie. If I have a fleeting conversation with someone I may never meet again, chances are I will not disclose this part of my family story. Under all other circumstances I will. I no longer worry whether this information is "too heavy," or whether it will create discomfort in my conversation partner. Like Tina, I "own" my story. Telling of my brother's suicide has, of course, turned out to be a supremely beautiful door. It always invites empathy. If my conversation partner has also known a person who has committed suicide, it facilitates that conversation!

TOSS THE OLD STORIES

We have all spoken with folks whose stories sound "old." We listen, and every phrase sounds rehearsed. The pauses become predictable. The jokes sound stale. The punch lines feel mechanical.

It can be actually marvelous to tell Moment and Meaning Stories, again and again. Inspirational leaders have an arsenal of such stories they draw on, at will. These are well-considered stories. They know the purpose of these stories. They know when to tell them, and they tell them well.

A Life Story told over and over again, however, can get "old" before we know it. If I first told this story ten years ago, I continue to tell it from the perspective of who I was, ten years ago. It's now a ten-year-old story. Because I live life every day and add new experiences and insights, the sense I make of the past will hopefully evolve, as well. My Writing Story, for example, is the story I may tell about how I write, my process of writing, the experience of getting published. I have had my Writing Story since back in the 90s, when I first began to write. This story changed when I wrote my book *Power Speaking*. My Writing Story is further evolving as I write *Infectious*. I jot down these words as I am completing this manuscript. Chances are, it will be a different story again as you read these words, well past the book's publication.

So please, keep your Life Stories fresh. Keep asking yourself if they continue to ring true. Don't become a time-warp storyteller.

FIVE STORYTELLING ESSENTIALS

The first three tips will serve you well when you tell a story:

1. **Know the purpose.**

   When I sit at a club and chatter away with my five best friends, any story will do. When I sit at a business dinner with colleagues or give a prepared speech, it may be helpful to know why I'm telling my story. In case of a prepared story, that is easily accomplished. In a formal setting, avoid second-guessing yourself but do a split-second gut check. It's a wonderful way of making sure that the story you're telling is advancing the conversation with purpose.

2. **Keep the background information simple.**

   All Moment Stories have impact because we take our conversation partner into the experience of that moment. The more time we take to create a context for this moment, the less interested my listener will be in the actual story. The story lives in the details of the moment, not in the details of the setup.

Meaning and Life Stories tend to be more cognitive, but the same guidance applies. Ramble your way through the meaning portion, and you will test your listener's patience. Meander through your life story, and they will quickly lose interest in your life. Get to your message or insight quickly. Explore the insight keenly and succinctly.

3. Paint a picture.

Stories "work" because they evoke an emotional response in the listener. The emotional response is caused by the details we tell.

When you refer to people and places, mention their names. They anchor and make the story "real." In my Moment Story, I made sure to mention the location of my camel experience—Petra—and my brother's name—Thomas. Even though you may not have been to Petra and likely have never met Thomas, you will have instant impressions of a place or person based on hearing the name.

Describe a place with a quick word or phrase. "The light inside the canyon was very murky and dark." "The canyon walls became so narrow that we were forced to ride single file." Those simple details allow you to be transported into my Petra story. They help to make the ride into the can-yon vivid. Chances are, the Petra you're seeing in your mind looks nothing like the Petra I experienced. It doesn't matter; you have fleshed out my story with your own imagination. That's a wondrous thing.

Describe the physical sensations within your story. "My skin was quivering from the cool air." "Water kept dripping from my body." Descriptions that involve our five senses allow our listeners to connect with their own memories of the five senses. These tend to be most potent and primal memories any of us have!

The next two tips aim to make sure you don't interfere with the emotional impact of a story.

4. Don't rush.

Many of us tend to not trust the details of a Moment Story. We worry that we're "taking too long." Instead of telling the story, we tell a high-level sketch of the story. By not trusting the details, we create the very thing we're trying to avoid; we make sure that the story really has no impact, or we diminish the impact it might have.

5. Don't over-explain.

The opposite pattern comes into play when we tell a Meaning or a Life Story. Because we don't trust our ability to tell it clearly, and we don't trust that our listener really "gets it," we explain it over and over and over. You may be familiar with the old adage "tell a message, tell it again, and then tell it a third time to make sure they really got it?" In the best of situations, this approach is an insult to our listeners. It truly doesn't work in storytelling. Tell it once—and then let it go.

PRINCIPLE #5: REFRAME THE CONVERSATION

You know the moment when we feel stuck in a conversation we don't wish to have, right? The stomach tightens, the throat feels tense, the mind starts racing. Our conversation partner is harping on a point that we no longer wish to debate. The vehemence of the other person is making us uncomfortable. We want to shift gears—but in that moment it simply seems impossible. We could certainly tell the other person that we don't want to talk about whatever it is we're talking about: the straight-shooting approach. We could exit the conversation altogether by excusing ourselves: the avoidance approach.

Both of these options work—once in a while. They work best when we have no stake in the relationship with our conversation partner. They are hardly ever an option in a formal business conversation.

Enter reframing.

Reframing is the subtle art of redirecting the flow of a conversation. An expert reframer takes a comment or idea that's "on the table" and shifts it in a new direction. He does so by asking a question. The question is strategic, and the nature of the question will define the flow of the conversation. Better yet—the technique we use as we reframe is entirely invisible. We know that we are strategically shifting a conversation, yet our conversation partner merely hears us asking a very pertinent question.

We reframe instinctively, all the time. At times we get lucky, and our question really does steer the conversation in a helpful direction. An expert reframer doesn't rely on luck. She knows what her potential reframing questions are—and she makes a deliberate choice.

Here are six simple techniques for reframing a conversation:

1. Widen the Lens

Sample statement	*There is way too much new building construction here at the beach.*
Reframing question	*How does the volume of construction at this beach compare to the volume in the rest of the country?*
Benefit	We take a narrowly focused observation and invite a broader reflection.

2. Narrow the Lens

Sample statement	*Television newscasts are biased and don't present information objectively.*
Reframing question	*Which aspect of these newscasts do you consider most subjective?*
Benefit	We take sweeping generalizations and invite a more focused reflection.

3. Contemplate the Opposite

Sample statement	*We keep streamlining our work processes, and all these changes make what I have to do more complicated!*
Reframing question	*What do you think would happen if we did not streamline and kept things just as they are?*
Benefit	We invite a deeper reflection upon the rationale for a controversial decision or action.

4. Switch from Problem to Solution

Sample statement	*These new company policy manuals are way too detailed and boring. Nobody will read them!*
Reframing question	*What changes would make these manuals more user-friendly?*
Benefit	We stop persistent complaining by inviting helpful suggestions.

5. Identify Barriers

Sample statement	*This is such an exciting project. I can't wait to get started and make all of this happen.*
Reframing question	*What are some potential challenges we may wish to consider before we begin?*
Benefit	We invite a deeper reflection on a situation when potential risk is involved.

6. Highlight an Underlying Issue

Sample statement	*We spend too much time in meetings bickering, trying to outdo each other, and going around in circles.*
Reframing question	*We seem to not fully trust each other. What is, in your opinion, causing this lack of trust?*
Benefit	We invite a reflection on the root causes of a difficult situation.

These techniques look pretty simple in writing; they're tougher to execute in the middle of a conversation. They will begin to feel seamless after repeated practice in a whole slew of different social situations. The following tips will help you to reframe with finesse. Some of these tips actively contradict guidance from our first four principles. Remember—the first four principles are about shifting "into" a conversation; the reframing principle is about shifting "away" from the present conversation.

Tip #1: Withhold Your Emotions.

We reframe because we wish to steer a conversation into a new direction. An emotional response to a comment we just heard, a sarcastic aside, a derogatory body movement—they all keep us stuck in the present conversation. Have your emotional response; don't show it when you're reframing!

Tip #2: Don't Use Invitational Language.

Invitational language within the flow of a conversation favorably acknowledges the comments we just heard. When we shift a conversation, we do not validate anything that was just said. We are merely asking a clean question that takes the conversation in a new direction.

Tip #3: Don't State Your Point of View.

Stating our point of view is an instant response to a comment we just heard. It will keep us in the conversation we are already having—it will not move us into a new conversation.

Tip #4: Keep It Short.

When we reframe a conversation, we want to do so efficiently. Don't babble, don't elaborate, don't ask the same question three times over. An effective reframing question is succinct. The longer the question, the less effective our reframing will be.

SUMMARY

Talk is the first of our Four Levels of Connection. It defines the most easily visible and audible part of our connection with others. It is, if you will, the surface of our social experience, the thing that others can most readily witness. If we don't engage with a measure of skill and ease at the Talk Level, we are actively inhibiting the possibility of resonating with anyone at a deeper level. We never get to experience an infectious connection!

Think of a conversation as an improvisational dance between two or more folks. Our comfort in engaging another person through talk is the tipping point in this delicate dance, the force that turns it into either a pleasurable romp or an ordeal we can't wait to escape. Five simple principles, and the skills that accompany these principles, help us to shape any chat into an improvisation that brims with warmth, substance, and emotional connection.

Principle #1: Invite Me In.

Email-writing and texting have turned us into bullet-pointed communicators. This efficient communication style is increasingly showing up in one-on-one conversations. Crisp is good; cool and uninviting is not. Entice your conversation partner. Use emotional cue words and language that draw him into a conversation with you.

Principle #2: Open the Doors.

A conversation is like a walk down a long hallway lined with closed doors. Each verbal cue we hear is an invitation to open a door. Be curious. Take a risk. Notice the doors. Choose to open them.

Principle #3: Have a Point of View.

Your point of view about an event, an experience, an idea helps me to better understand you. When you state your viewpoint, you invite me to share my viewpoint in turn. It immediately enriches our conversation. Use language that clearly signals your point of view, and let your conversation partner off the hook by making it OK for her to have an entirely different perspective.

Principle #4: Own Your Stories.

Stories are a powerful way of conveying what truly matters to us. They are also a thrilling means of creating an emotional bond with others. We tend to tell three different types of stories: Moment Stories, Meaning Stories, Life Stories. Stories have impact when they are told well. Know the purpose of your story, trust the details, and do not over-explain.

Principle #5: Reframe the Conversation.

When we find ourselves in a conversation that seems to be going nowhere, we can leave—or we can reframe the conversation. Artful reframing is invisible to our conversation partner yet elegantly shifts the direction of our chat. It shows a true mastery of the moment. Each of the six reframing questions in this chapter creates a uniquely different shift in conversation. Master talkers strategically choose their reframing questions as they shape their conversations.

Chapter 3

Level Two: Power Is Real

Four Levels of Connection

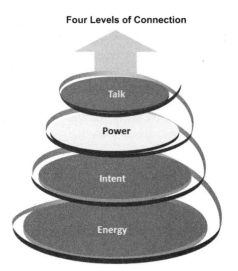

Table 3: Our second level of connection

I remember a conversation I had back in 2003. I was writing a book called *Power Speaking,* and I was floating my idea for the book's title by Bruce Morris, then a columnist for the Sunday Styles section in the *New York Times.* "Huhhm," Bruce declared with off-the-cuff disdain. "The word 'power' is passé. Everyone wants something more spiritual these days."

His comment touched a nerve in me. I view myself as a spiritual person, so what the heck did I really mean when I used the word "power?" Did I have a lot of unexamined notions about this thing called power? I wasn't thinking about ego, bravado, manipulation—that I knew. I wasn't thinking of folks like Donald Trump who flaunt power like an oversized diamond ring. I certainly wasn't thinking of it as a throwback to the discover-your-personal-power liberation movements of the '60s and '70s. So—what *was* I thinking of?

Back then I had never seen a power model—but the moment I did, I had my quintessential "aha" moment. So there was a way to take the elusive notion of "power" and break it into specific power factors! All my ruminations about power suddenly made sense to me. I hope the same will be true for you. In the meantime, here is a story or two to set the stage.

I flash back to an afternoon in the summer of 1976. I am walking up Via Veneto in Rome, enraptured by the rich history of this wonderful city, a history that seems to seep out of the pores of every building I pass. The moment I am about to describe is like a cliché from a Fellini movie—except that it really happened. As I am strolling up the Via, Ursula Andress is descending toward me. Even before I see her I notice people ahead of me suddenly step aside. It's as if I am witnessing the proverbial parting of the seas. Ms. Andress, the original Bond girl, is strolling down the Via with a strong, firm gait, her head held high, her posture erect, her celebrated bosom thrust forward with an easy confidence. She is tall, a fact that's accentuated by her proud and elongated carriage. Her prominent bone structure lends her face a ferocious beauty. As Ms. Andress gets closer and closer—and just as quickly passes me by—I sense that "thing" that I am often asked to coach people on. I sense presence. I sense animal magnetism. I sense charisma. I couldn't really name it then—but, yes, I sense personal power. Oodles and oodles of personal power.

Since we will excavate the elements of power in this portion of the book, let me break down the obvious ones that Ms. Andress exuded: She had the power of fame (position). She had the power of beauty (body). She had the power of animal magnetism (charisma). But more importantly, in that public walk down Via Veneto, Ursula Andress "owned" her power. She didn't shrivel. She didn't apologize. She wrapped herself in her power and at the same time tossed it to the wind.

Did this power help Ms. Andress connect with folks? Hardly. Ms. Andress remained an aloof object of admiration and desire. I trust that this was her intent. In this walk, Ms. Andress wasn't looking to connect—she was just looking to part the seas.

Let's ratchet up the position power a notch or two. It is October of 1999, and I stand in the corner of a small reception room inside the Grand Park Hotel, the only five-star accommodation in Ramallah, Palestine. Shimon Peres enters the room. His Center for Peace is one of the producers of a theater project that features a cast of Jordanian, Palestinian, and Israeli actors. I am the director of the production. It is minutes before the first performance of this play in the Palestinian territories, and Mr. Peres is showing up for a quick meet-and-greet with Israeli and Palestinian dignitaries. He is flanked by two bodyguards and a press secretary. As his press secretary guides him toward certain guests, Mr. Peres starts to engage.

I notice it at once. The energy in the room changes the moment Mr. Peres enters. It happens whenever people with exceptional power enter a space. Mr. Peres has megawatt position power, and he arrives with the symbol of such power—his entourage. The entire social dance in this little room instantly revolves around this immovable truth.

Here's the part that gets my attention, though. As I stand in my corner and observe, I watch Mr. Peres engage. No surprise— he is in total command of the engagement skills we examined in the preceding chapter. He has done this a zillion times. But there's power, and then there's what we do with it. I notice the grace with which Mr. Peres moves through the room. He is unhurried, even though his time is limited. He comfortably holds the gaze of everyone with whom he speaks. He pauses thoughtfully. He follows up with questions. Each encounter seems easy and unforced. As fleeting as these moments are, Mr. Peres is fully present.

Mr. Peres wants to connect.

This is the most basic—but not so simple—power question: How do I "own" my power? How do I "wear" it? How does it wear me? When I pose this question in one of my seminars, most participants don't quite know what I mean. This still startles me, every time. Mr. Peres knows how to own his power. The way I answer this question will instantly change the way I connect with absolutely anyone. There's an equally compelling second part to this question: How do I relate to the power of others? Imagine being in a room alone with Ms. Andress. How would you interact with her? Or alone with Mr. Peres, the bodyguards banished?

LEARNING THE POWER LESSONS

I like celebrity examples because they push hidden power dynamics to the surface. They make everything that is invisible— yet always there—absolutely plain and clear. Here's a moment that taught me my very own power lesson. Twice in the mid-nineties I had the good fortune to be invited out to Montauk, at the far eastern end of Long Island, to be a guest at The Barn. The Barn is a building that is true to its name—it really is an old barn-turned-guesthouse. Edward Albee, the American playwright who wrote the classic *Who's Afraid of Virginia Woolf?* and many other great plays, owns The Barn. Each summer his foundation invites six artists—painters, sculptors, writers—to come out for a month, live at The Barn, and work on a creative project.

Mr. Albee lived a couple of miles away, right on the Atlantic, and each morning he would pick up the mail at the post office in Montauk and deliver it to the residents at The Barn. I would sit in my tiny quarters right above the living-room and invariably, some-time toward late morning, hear the rattling of Mr. Albee's beat-up old Mercedes as it hurtled down the driveway. I would run down to the kitchen to say hello and see if there was any mail for me. My encounters with Mr. Albee were always awkward. Our conversations felt stilted and rushed. Mr. Albee seemed ever so shy and sullen to me, or quite possibly downright misanthropic.

Or so I thought—until my friend Orison Aguayo came out for a visit.

Orison happened to be standing with me on the deck outside of the kitchen as Edward Albee arrived with the mail. I introduced Orison to Mr. Albee. Orison—vivacious, hyper-chatty—immediately started to talk to Edward Albee about something or other. I don't remember what they chatted about, I just know that it was nothing at all consequential. But the conversation flowed. Edward Albee was animated. His eyes twinkled with delight. He guffawed loudly, which I had not heard him do before. He seemed to have a grand old time.

That's when I understood. Like the other residents at The Barn, I put Edward Albee on a pedestal. He was *the* great living American playwright. He was my benefactor. I was star-struck. I bowed to his power and didn't own any of my own. No wonder Edward Albee did not enjoy speaking with me. Orison, on the other hand, was fearless. He fully owned one of his key sources of power—the ability to strike up a conversation with anyone—and went at it with Edward Albee. They had a blast!

WHY POWER MATTERS

I trust this intuitively makes sense: People who connect well understand their own power and use it effectively. They're also not easily cowed by the powers of others. We all have at some point or other used the phrase that someone "plays well with others." I prefer the notion that someone "plays well with the power of others." That's what Orison did.

Personal power is the second level at which connections either happen or don't (Table 3). If I am not connected with my power at this level, it will diminish the impact of the third and fourth levels at which we connect: our Intent and our Energy. To put it in the simplest terms, if I am disconnected from myself, how can I possibly connect with you? And why the heck would you want to connect with me?

So how do I connect with myself? In this chapter we will take the notion of power and ascribe it to five distinct sources (Table 4: Power Plugs model by Achim Nowak and Dr. Margarita Gurri). Our position. Our expertise. Our relationships. Our body. And our charisma. I will use the term "power plug" to describe these sources. I view charisma as the central power plug and the other four as ancillary but equally powerful ones. Just as we light up a dark room by plugging into a light source, the word "plug" suggests that a personal source of power is available to me. It also implies that I need to consciously connect with it. Plug in. My ability to tap these sources of power defines how I "show up," how I speak up, and the substance of my engagement with others.

Power Plugs

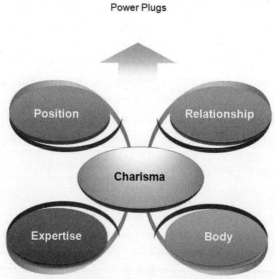

Table 4: Our Five Power Plugs

Couple this with my ability to tap into the power plugs of my conversation partner(s), and suddenly we're dancing in the invisible world.

I. POWER PLUGS BAROMETER

Before we jump into this section, please take a quick climate check to see how you relate to the five power plugs. It's simple, and I hope it will not only stimulate your thoughts about your social habits but further pique your interest in the power plugs.

In each of the following ten tables you will find three statements that describe potential attitudes and behaviors in a social situation. Take a look at each statement. Distribute a total of ten points among all three statements within a table. You must allot all ten points but may distribute them in any way you wish. This may mean that they end up being distributed somewhat evenly (Example 1), entirely unevenly (Example 2), or in any other configuration that adds up to ten!

Example 1:

I. *When I meet people for the first time . . .*

1.	*I like to convey my passion and enthusiasm for what matters to me.*	3
2.	*I can find something interesting in pretty much anyone.*	3
3.	*I make sure I look and feel my best.*	4

Example 2:

I. *When I meet people for the first time . . .*

1.	*I like to convey my passion and enthusiasm for what matters to me.*	9
2.	*I can find something interesting in pretty much anyone.*	0
3.	*I make sure I look and feel my best.*	1

There is no perfect or desirable distribution of points, so don't overthink this activity. Key is that you allot ten points in each table. Move through this activity quickly and have fun with it!!!

I.   When I meet people for the first time . . .

1. I like to convey my passion and enthusiasm for what matters to me.	
2. I can find something interesting in pretty much anyone.	
3. I make sure I look and feel my best.	

II.   What I respond to most in other people is . . .

1. Their knowledge and wisdom.	
2. Their personal energy.	
3. Their playful sense of humor.	

III. This is what I am most likely to tell my very close friends . . .

1. New information and ideas that excite me.	
2. The challenges I experience in my work life.	
3. My personal joys and sorrows.	

IV. This is what I am most likely to NOT tell even my very close friends:

1. Problems in an intimate personal relationship.	
2. Anxiety over a major physical ailment.	
3. A major setback at work.	

V. What I most like about myself is that . . .

1. I am able to make a difference in the world.	
2. I am vital and attractive.	
3. I usually know what I am talking about.	

VI. As I get older, I want to make sure I . . .

1. Look back with satisfaction on what I have accomplished in my life.	
2. Am fit to do what I want.	
3. Have learned from my mistakes.	

VII. In a business meeting, I get satisfaction out of . . .

1. Involving the entire group.	
2. Getting things done.	
3. Motivating and inspiring folks.	

VIII. At a party, I get satisfaction out of meeting . . .

1. The really sharp-looking people.	
2. The really smart people.	
3. The really vibrant and dynamic people.	

IX. When folks talk about me, they are likely to say that . . .

1. They can't wait to hang out with me.	
2. They love my fire and spunk.	
3. They admire what I have done with my life.	

X. The following makes me want to connect more deeply with someone:

1. The person bursts with energy.	
2. The person is easy on the eye.	
3. The person is super-smart.	

Great!!! Now simply transfer all your points from the preceding ten tables into the Barometer Reading.

Transfer tip: Take a look at your responses in your first table. Transfer your points from this table into the empty boxes in the first row of our barometer. If you, for example, awarded nine points to the first statement, transfer nine points to the CH box. If you awarded zero points to the second statement, transfer zero points to the RE box. And if you awarded one point to the third statement, transfer one point to the BO box. Continue this process for the remaining nine tables!

YOUR POWER PLUGS BAROMETER READING

Table	PO Position Power	RE Relationship Power	EX Expert Power	BO Body Power	CH Charisma Power
I.		2.		3.	1.
II.		3.	1.		2.
III.	2.	3.	1.		
IV.	3.	1.		2.	
V.	1.		3.	2.	
VI.	1.		3.	2.	

VII	2.	1.			3.
VIII.			2.	1.	3.
IX.	3.	1.			2.
X.			3.	2.	1.
TOTAL POINTS					

PO is your Position Power.
RE is your Relationship Power.
EX is your Expertise Power.
BO is your Body Power.
CH is your Charisma. Power.
And here, my friend, is your Power Plugs Weather Forecast!

POWER PLUGS WEATHER FORECAST

Points	Temperature	Implications
30 or more	Burning Hot	**This plug is mega-charged.** It drives your behavior in absolutely every social situation. Others need to engage with it well, or they don't stand a chance with you.

23-29	Soothing Warm	**This plug is charged.** You plug into it easily. You play well with others who also plug into this power within themselves. You like it when others play well with this power source.
16-22	Slight Chill	**This plug is mildly charged.** You are plugged in here but you're not highly charged. This power source is likely a bit underutilized. Plug into it more often, and be surprised by the sparks it will create in your relationships.
15 or less	Arctic Cold	**This plug doesn't get your engine running.** It could be that you just don't care—or that you have oodles of it and take it for granted. If someone tries too hard to plug in here, you can switch off fast.

Any **Burning Hot** Power Plug has the potential of shutting down the circuit boards around us. While we're plugged in here, others around us may be ready to tune us out. Any **Arctic Cold** Power Plug will benefit from a more deliberate charge by us. Chances are, if we charge up more deliberately here, we will invite more robust and resonant connections with others.

In the upcoming pages, we'll take a close peek at each of the Five Power Plugs. Every Power Plug section ends with Five Tips on how to better charge this power plug. Finally, we'll look at specific ways of better connecting with the Power Plugs of the folks we engage with. So—let's get charged!

II. POSITION POWER

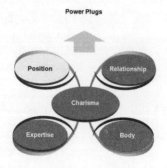

Position power is the power that is awarded us through our function at work, our professional role, or the social status we have inherited. No matter how much we dress it up with fancy language, at its core it means that we have the power to reward folks we like and ignore or punish folks we don't. Even when this power is clear, knowing how to use it never is. It can confound those individuals who possess it, and it can be equally confounding to anyone who engages with the individual who has it.

Here's an impromptu chat I had with Stuart Perkins, the previously mentioned CEO of a global manufacturing company.

"Do you have a few minutes?" Stuart asks me as I pass him in the hallway of his company's corporate headquarters in Chicago. Every communication interests me, even the way such a simple question is phrased. Stuart asks it beautifully, he is that kind of a guy. Affable. Drily funny at times. Comfortable with his power, and deeply respectful of others.

"Nobody talks to me anymore."

Stuart says it tongue-in-cheek as we pull shut the door of a little conference room. He has a twinkle in his eye as he speaks, but I know there's truth in his statement.

Stuart had just stopped by a breakfast gathering for a group of mid-level managers who were in Chicago to attend a training program. It was a surprise drop-in. Stuart wanted to chat, ask a few questions, welcome employees he'd never met. He was going way beyond the call of duty.

Stuart spoke. The managers were silent and did not say a peep.

For a connector like Stuart, this was deeply unsettling. "They are a little afraid of you, Stuart," I say to him. "You're the CEO." He is silent. I am not always right, but I'm pretty sure that's what was going on there. Stuart had just stepped into the age-old "it's lonely at the top" scenario.

WHAT WE FEAR WHEN "THE OTHER" HAS POSITION POWER

What are we really afraid of with position holders? Even with a guy like Stuart who seems to be genuinely approachable? Each time I ponder this question, I end up with the same three beliefs. These beliefs apply regardless of the social context in which we meet the person.

1. Their time is too valuable.
2. They won't find what I have to say interesting.
3. If I say the wrong thing there will be a price to pay.

These beliefs define the infinite playground of position-power-fear. They kick into gear even in the face of evidence to the contrary. Stuart's time wasn't too valuable—he had made a point of dropping by. He was asking questions because he really did want to hear what his managers had to say. It didn't matter. At the bottom of our silence is the fear that we are not enough. And this fear has nothing at all to do with the other person's position power.

This drop-into-fear ritual occurs in nearly every social setting, even when the other person has no immediate power over us whatsoever. The singer Marianne Faithfull writes about it beautifully in her memoir *Faithfull*. It is the spring of 1965. Ms. Faithfull is eighteen years old and just had a big hit with her song "As Tears Go By," written by Mick Jagger. She is the it-girl of the moment in the British pop scene. And then she suddenly finds herself in Bob Dylan's hotel room at the Savoy Hotel in London, hanging out with glitterati like Allen Ginzberg and Joan Baez and, of course, Mr. Dylan.

> I was completely overwhelmed by this very cool guy on lots of methedrine, and I didn't want to be the first to make a foolish move. After all, he had a reputation for being incredibly nasty. My throat was dry, my mind seized up. I mean, what if I said something really stupid? The gates of Eden would be closed forever. I was, naturally, unable to speak. I just sat there trying to look beautiful. If I so much as opened my mouth in this rarefied atmosphere, I was bound to sound inane. They were all so hip, so devastatingly hip.[7]

It's a safe bet that every day that year, person after person who met Marianne Faithfull was equally tongue-tied when speaking with her. And it's a 100% guaranteed that unless we examine our own power stories, we will create one Marianne Faithfull moment after another in our social encounters.

THE POWER STORIES WE CARRY WITH US

We learn about how we relate to position power when we are young. I grew up in a world in which position power mattered a great deal. It wasn't just inferred—it was visible on a daily basis. In the late 1960s, when my family lived in Ankara, a protestant minister came once a month from Istanbul to lead a German-language service in a reception hall at the embassy. My parents didn't much care for religion. We went because—well, that's what everyone else did once a month when the minister came! Even in church this much was clear: Folks sat according to rank. The ambassador and his family sat in the front row. The cultural attaché sat a row or two behind them. The chancellor, head of the lower echelons of the embassy staff, sat somewhere in the middle of the room. And my family sat a few rows behind the chancellor.

I got the idea.

When we conversed with someone who sat in the front rows, we waited for them to approach us. We said little, volunteered even less, and limited ourselves to answering their questions. We demurred.

A special reverence was reserved for descendants of German nobility. In Germany, those folks carry the letters "von" in front of their surname. Anyone can spot a descendant of German nobility, or someone who has married into nobility, simply by hearing the person's name. We had a few of the "vons" at the German embassy. And no, I'm not making this up: Mom actually lowered her voice into a near-stage whisper when she mentioned their names. It was as if we were blessed to simply breathe the same air they exhaled. Within the confines of power and status, the nobles lived in an exalted plane that eluded us and everyone else.

My lesson was pretty clear: We spoke differently to folks who had social or position power. We deferred to them, always. I have no memory of those folks speaking differently to us. Maybe they did—but it was really all about how we behaved. Yes, this was wholly the inside job within my family.

What you just read is part of my personal power narrative, drilled deep into my psyche. You have your own. We all have it. If we're fortunate, it was stated explicitly. Most of us just inhaled it as if by osmosis. That's when it really kicks our behinds. It is there, all the time, and it writes the script for every social encounter we have.

WHAT WE FEAR WHEN WE HAVE POSITION POWER

The other day I stumbled onto a re-run of the TV-show *Super-nanny*. Watching just a few minutes of this guilty pleasure reminded me of every parent I have observed who seems to not have a clue of how to talk to his child. Parents, after all, have loads of very clear position power. I can get quite annoyed when I listen to a

INFECTIOUS

parent who talks to her children in regressive baby-babble, as if the child had no IQ. I can get annoyed at the parent who is letting his child run wild without ever setting a limit. I can get annoyed at the parent who is constantly chiding her child—a chiding which seems to only fuel the behavior the parent is trying to curb.

I may get annoyed, but I empathize with the underlying challenge every parent is trying to figure out: How do I use my position power in a way that creates a helpful relationship with my child? How do I connect with my child when I receive so many conflicting messages about what good parenting looks like?

The same questions arise the moment we have any sort of position power and engage with others. I often work with business leaders who are newly thrust into a Senior VP or CEO role. Much like a new parent, every one of them quickly starts to grapple with questions he had not fully considered before. That's a good thing. I worry about anyone with Position Power who doesn't contemplate these questions:

1. Who can I really trust? What can I tell whom, and how will I know that it remains confidential?
2. When I play with the other alpha boys and alpha girls who also have lots of position power—how much of the time do I take up with my thoughts and ideas, and how much of the time do I listen to what they have to say?
3. When am I talking too much? When am I not talking enough?
4. How do I stay approachable when there really is never enough time to talk to anybody?
5. How do I speak about my professional life when I am not in my professional role? How do I switch with ease from a role with lots of position power into the other social roles in my life?

Do any of these questions sound familiar? I hope they do. I do not have tidy answers for us—the answers to these questions will be very personal and defined by our unique social circumstances. But the moment we engage in a dialogue with these questions we're beginning to play with power in a more conscious manner. And that's very helpful, indeed.

FIVE WAYS TO BETTER PLUG INTO YOUR POSITION POWER

Here are some concrete ways in which you can fully own your position power. These simple behaviors will be instantly visible to others. Moreover, folks will appreciate these behaviors and connect with you with a fuller appreciation of your position power:

1. **Be comfortable saying "yes" or "no" and setting limits.**
   People with position power know they cannot be everything to everybody. They know how to not say "yes" to ideas and suggestions that do not feel right to them. They know to not make commitments they cannot keep. They have learned to do this with kindness and without being dismissive of others. Their ease and clarity invites the same ease and clarity in others.

2. **Trust your gut instinct when you speak.**
   When we trust our gut instinct we advance a conversation to a higher degree of honesty. Our gut instinct does not mean we're right—it simply means we're willing to stop censoring our conversations with others and take a risk.

3. **Enjoy stating your point of view.**
   We have explored point of view language in a previous chapter. The operative word here is "enjoy." When I delight in stating a point of view, I infuse this sense of delight into the entire conversation. And a delighted conversation frequently turns into a memorable one.

4. **Invite disagreement.**
   I demonstrate comfort with my position power when I encourage a diversity of opinions in a conversation. Because others may judiciously edit themselves around me, I advance the conversation when I actively solicit a point of view that may be different from mine.

5. Take charge of situations with ease.

In situations where you are expected to make a decision, small or large—make the decision. Others will respect you for your ease with this aspect of your position power.

III. RELATIONSHIP POWER

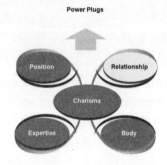

I picked up the best-selling book *Never Eat Alone* because I loved the title. I enjoyed its chatty writing style. And then, as I kept reading on, I found myself getting pretty darn angry. The author, Keith Ferrazzi, prides himself on having over 5,000 people in his database. These 5,000 folks are touted as examples of successful relationships. Success is defined as having access to people with influence who can be helpful to us. The distinguishing success factor? These 5,000 folks will pick up the phone and speak to Mr. Ferrazzi when he calls, without passing him off to a screener or handler. Relationships, in Mr. Ferrazi's world, are business commodities.

Once I calmed down, I had to admit that Mr. Ferrazzi had a point. Access to people is real power. It is one facet of relationship power. There are a whole bunch of folks who were helpful in getting this book published. The fact that I had people I could call for help at different stages of the publishing process was vital. Without such access, my journey of seeing this book through to publication might have felt a lot more daunting.

SUSTAINING OUR RELATIONSHIPS

What I value most in my professional and personal life, however, is the ability to sustain a relationship over time. As my circle of relationships has widened, that is not a given. Circumstances, in fact, every day conspire against doing just that. There are friends and colleagues who I cherish greatly but who, because of our busy lives, I get to see in person only after long intervals. One of my markers for a powerful relationship is the effortlessness with which we slip in and out of each other's lives. When we can pick up where we had left off, with the same sense of intimacy, as if no time had passed at all.

I think of my friend Ellen MacDonald, a painter turned therapist who I have known since our early artist days in the bohemian subculture of Washington, DC. Our connection spans from creating sets for an experimental theater production to snorkeling in Tobago to late-night chats in her loft in Brooklyn to Ellen's wedding last summer, on a grassy promontory in the Catskills. A ruthless honesty about our respective life lessons is the glue that holds this relationship together.

I think of Kit Williams, a colleague and mentor who I have had the good fortune to work with in her multiple incarnations as a Leadership Development master. The respect we have for each other's talents, coupled with an easy rapport about personal interests that transcend professional pleasantry, is the connector.

I think of Jim Mirrione, a playwright and frequent theatre collaborator with whom I have traveled from theatre festivals in Vancouver to community centers in the South Bronx to play rehearsals in the Israeli desert to strolls through the campus of Al Ain University in the United Arab Emirates where Jim now teaches. A shared sense of adventure and an appreciation of the expatriate life keep bringing us back together.

What makes it possible to drop in and out of these relationships? At some point, these colleagues and I established a connection potent enough that it compelled us to drop in, again and again.

How do I know that I have one of those connections? It starts with the feeling of anticipatory joy right before I get to see you again. The "I can't wait to have dinner with you" joy. The "I will move mountains to see you again" joy. The "We don't need to have any plans let's just hang" kind of joy.

There is "juice" in these relationships.

How did we get the juice? Right from the start, all of the skills we explored in the Talk chapter came into play. These skills unfolded with a measure of grace. Without the Talk skills, all of our connections are forever relegated to a light appetizer on the relationship menu instead of the grand five-course meal.

DEVELOPING A "RELATIONSHIP RANGE"

When I think of Ellen and Kit and Jim, I also think of the ability to be "in relationship" with each other in many different ways. The ability to be in silence with someone while in the same room. The ability to ferociously brainstorm in a business meeting. The ability to have a cordial relationship with people I don't like all that much. The ability to disagree with passion and sincere respect. The ability to get senselessly silly. The ability to embrace another person's mood. The ability to go with the flow in any conversation.

When I was an acting coach we called this "having a range." It describes the ability of an actor to inhabit a wide range of characters and situations. The worst thing you can say to an actor is that he doesn't have a range. Nobody wants to hire an actor without a range. Even highly seasoned actors study and continue to study with an acting coach to explore and expand their range. Well, life is our relationship school. When it works, it teaches us our own wide range of "being in relationship." So, celebrate the opportunities each relationship offers you to help expand your relationship range. What great fun that can be!

At the core of this range is our sincere desire to actually be "in relationship." Now—we may want to protest, at once. Well, of course I want to be in relationship! But think about it. How many times have we been in a business meeting and did not wish to be in relationship with "those" folks (I can think of a moment or two . . .)? How many times did we have a chat with a colleague in the hallway and did not wish to be in relationship with "that" person (I can think of a moment or two . . .)? How many times did we chat with someone at a party and did not wish to be in relationship with "that" person (I can think of a moment or two . . .)? How many times . . . well, I trust the point is clear! Yes, I have my moments when I just don't wish to relate to anyone. If those moments proliferate, however, there's a good chance I don't intend to be in relationship with anyone, period. (More about intent in our next chapter.) If this intent is habitually lacking, I have already abdicated my relationship power. And in the long haul, that surely diminishes my ability to have true impact in the world!

FIVE WAYS TO BETTER PLUG INTO YOUR RELATIONSHIP POWER

Here are some simple and very specific ways in which you can instantly enhance your own Relationship Power.

1. **Initiate contact with strangers.**
   In any situation where there is an opportunity to meet someone new, be the initiator. At a party, go up to folks you don't know. On an airplane, strike up a chat with your travel companion. At a networking function, stop hanging out with the buddies you came with. If you don't do any of this habitually, jump over your own shadow and just do it!

2. **Take pleasure in telling others about yourself.**
   Instead of being a responder to the information others volunteer, volunteer information that helps us to better understand you. Healthy boundaries are great—but the more you tell us about experiences that are significant for you and ideas that excite you, the more we will care about you.

3. Choose to be interested in others.

People who are genuinely interested in other people have chosen to do so. They know that their curiosity will yield tremendous relationship rewards. Choose to be interested, and choose to do it sincerely. Anything less than that diminishes your relationship power.

4. Make people feel good.

This does not mean being a people-pleasing, phony-baloney cheerleader. But please—offer compliments that are heartfelt. Show appreciation whenever possible. Go the extra mile as often as possible. Do it, and your relationship rewards will be tremendous!

5. Stay in touch with people you know.

We abdicate relationship power every time we have social amnesia. You know, the moments when we don't answer emails, don't return phone calls, don't thank folks for their kindness, don't remember a milestone in another person's life. If we do this habitually, we are wasting precious social currency. Beware—this currency is not easily earned the second time around.

IV. EXPERTISE POWER

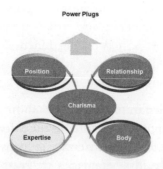

A great way to appreciate expertise power is to think of a moment when we didn't have it.

I remember teaching a class on "How to Design Web-based Training." A three-day course, and I was supposed to be the expert. I wasn't. I felt like a fraud. It was a truly horrible feeling. No matter how much I prepared, I just couldn't master this content. I was certain that most of my students knew more about this material than I did. My anxiety rose every night before I had to teach this class. My fear of being found out made me break out in hives. It was awful.

I taught this class over a period of months, and guess what—I did quite well! For a while. Then the moment came when someone asked a question that I couldn't answer. A very simple and basic question.

I called my bosses first thing the next morning and told them I couldn't teach this program even one more time. How liberating that phone call was. It set me free in so many ways. It released me of the fear of being found out. I no longer feel the need to know everything. I don't ever pretend to know what I don't know. This very call prompted one of the four guiding mantras in my firm: "We *know* what we're talking about." What matters more is the inverse of this statement. If we don't know, we don't pretend to know. We simply will not take the job—we'll send our client to someone else.

So let me state, for a moment, some of what I do know. I know coaching. I know training. I know growing a business. I know renovating a house. I know directing plays. I know writing. I know water. I know adventure. I know healing. I know friendship. I know love.

This is not meant to be a cocky list. Writing such a list brings up all the doubts I have about my areas of expertise. There may be better coaches, more brilliant writers, more dazzling public speakers, greater lovers. It's easy to compare and despair. There is a continuum of knowledge in every area I just mentioned. There will, I hope, always be a lot more for me to learn, yet I'm quite comfortable claiming a measure of expertise on this list.

Here's where expertise gets a little more complex, however. Yes, we may claim it, but what do we actually do with our expertise? How do we show it? How do we talk about it? I remember an off-the-cuff comment by my colleague Dawn Denvir, the Chief of Organizational Learning and Development at UNICEF: "They want us to be the expert, and they resent us for being the expert." That's the quintessential expertise dilemma, isn't it?

DOING THE EXPERT TALK

Here are some mental traps that oh-so-easily come into play as we toy with how to show our knowledge and expertise:

1. Are you a knowledge minimizer?

You don't wish to dominate situations with your knowledge. You don't wish others to feel inadequate because they know less. You worry that others will be intimidated by all that you know. So you withhold information in order to be liked.

2. Are a knowledge hoarder?

You fear that the more you tell, the more you give your power away. If you tell them everything, you will have no power left at all. So you withhold, and your knowledge remains your tightly guarded secret.

3. Are you a knowledge competitor?

When others share their expertise, you feel a compelling need to share yours. The urge to match their expertise just seems to take over. You don't mean to compete with their expertise—but you fear that if you don't, you will become irrelevant.

4. Are you a knowledge inflater?

You often find yourself in situations where you feel like you should know more than you do. Admitting that you don't know something seems utterly unbearable. So you habitually pretend to have more knowledge than you actually do.

True knowledge and expertise which remain unexpressed ulti-mately have little meaning. So while we ponder how to best express it in our professional and personal relationships, its deepest value resides in how we use it to be helpful to others. Our place of work offers us formal vehicles for doing so—by simply performing our job well, engaging every day with a sense of purpose, mentor-ing new colleagues, volunteering information, helping our busi-ness succeed. People with lots of expertise power also seem to be marvelously adept at finding venues outside of work where their expertise can be of service.

The ones who do it best do so with great humility.

AVOID ARRESTED DEVELOPMENT

To know what I don't know is a spot of marvelous power. It can open up surprising lines of conversation.

Our relationship to a city—any city—is an apt metaphor for the depth of learning that is possible. When I visit a city for the very first time, I like to buy a guide book, study it voraciously, search the web for any tidbits I can find. I don't like to not know, and I yearn to quickly get to the place of knowing. But the moment I actually step foot in this new city I lay full claim to being the first-time visitor. I ask the concierge at the hotel for help. I ask strangers on the street. I ask the taxi driver, the wait person, the street vendor, the tour guide. And with every question I not only deepen my knowledge and understanding of this new place but also create a potentially delicious connection with folks I did not previously know.

When we have lived in a city for a while, however, it is easy to settle into a state of arrested development. I know Hollywood, Florida—the city I call home—reasonably well. Yet here, as eve-rywhere else, I exist on a continuum of knowledge. I know it way better than I did eight years ago when I first got here. I certainly know it better than the first-time Canadian tourist who checks into a guest house at the beach. I don't know it nearly as well as my neighbors who were born here. Because a city is a growing organism, my knowledge of this city has to continue to grow, as well. New restaurants open, old ones close. New buildings rise, others are torn down. New people show up. New leaders put forth new ideas. New regulations change how business is conducted. So while I feel like I know Hollywood, I have the chance to rediscover it again, day in, day out. Very cool.

Expertise power gone wrong is the expertise where a sense of discovery has stopped. Do you remember a moment when you chatted with someone at a party and you realized that the person was stuck in a time warp? He is smart and educated and "knows his stuff," yet every reference he makes indicates that he is living in an earlier decade. His learning seems to have come to a crashing halt about ten years ago. Yes, arrested. Ouch. The moment I notice this, his outdated expertise becomes a liability. Instead of inviting a richer connection, it discourages it. This power plug is suddenly slammed shut!

FIVE WAYS TO BETTER PLUG INTO YOUR EXPERTISE POWER

Here are some wonderful ways in which you can fully appreciate and express your Relationship Power.

1. **Claim what you know—with humility.**

    We don't do anyone a service by not sharing our knowledge, wisdom, and expertise. Have a healthy sense of social context, but avoid the mental traps we reviewed in this section.

2. **Hang out with people who appreciate your expertise.**

    Friends who don't appreciate your expertise likely don't "get" your passions and dreams. Colleagues who don't appreciate your expertise don't "get" your true value. If you are surrounded by too many folks who don't "get you," move on. Our connections will always be severely limited when our expertise is not honored.

3. Find joy in bouncing ideas off other people.

When we run ideas, opinions, and solutions by other folks, it forces us to share our knowledge and expertise with them. Invite their feedback. Urge them to share their ideas, as well. Do so in professional and social settings—it is a marvelous way of making your invisible gifts visible to the world.

4. Be of service.

I hope this is a no-brainer. Every time I decide to be of service to others, I get to share part of my knowledge and expertise with them. I get to use what I know for a higher purpose—and I strengthen my relationship power along the way.

5. Conduct an Expertise Power Exercise
Write two lists:

1. My What I Know List (my areas of expertise, similar to the list I shared with you earlier in this section)
2. My What I Don't Know List (my areas of no expertise)

Some tips:

- Don't "sweat" this exercise. Go with your gut responses and jot them down. Do not take more than ten minutes to write each list.
- Notice the feelings that bubble up as you write your "What I Know List." They will offer you keen insights into how you value your expertise.
- Notice the feelings that bubble up as you write your "What I Don't Know List." They will offer you keen insights into the sort of expertise you value, and the ways in which you compare yourself to the expertise of others.
- As the cliché goes: The process of writing it down is as important as what you write down. Your insights will be your personal reward for this writing activity. What ends up on your list will likely be secondary!

V. BODY POWER

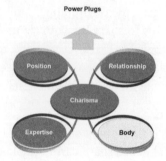

Before I started my own firm, I was a trainer for one of the largest train-the-trainer companies in the world. Two experiences stand out for me from that period of my life. When I was first hired by Langevin Learning Services, I lived in the East Village of Manhattan, the vibrant and eclectic counterpart to the city's more stately West Village. I was barely two weeks or so into my new job, hurrying down East Seventh Street toward Astor Place to catch the #6 train, when I passed the iron gate of an old tenement building. A voice behind the gate hissed at me: "Yuppie scum."

I was wearing my basic corporate garb—dress slacks, pressed shirt, tie. I looked polished.

The hiss was vicious.

At Langevin, clients evaluated my performance on a daily basis. It was the first time in my life that I received weekly "scores" for my work. My evaluations, thank goodness, were solid from the very start. In the evaluation forms there was, however, a small section that solicited additional feedback. Soon, this comment began to appear: "He needs a haircut." It was always followed by the words "just kidding." I realized right away that the folks who wrote this comment were not kidding—my haircut really did bother them, and they took the time to jot it down. Roughly once a month, another comment about my haircut appeared in my evaluations. Different people, same comment. I figured that for every person who jotted this down, there had to be three or four others who had a similar thought but refrained from commenting. My haircut seemed to annoy a lot of people!

Lest you wonder—I wore longish hair that fell to just below my ears. Washed and well-tended, of course.

I give my bosses at Langevin a lot of credit for not asking me to cut my hair. I did it on my own, a few years later; I simply didn't want my haircut to be a barrier any more. Yes, as I was juggling my downtown lifestyle with my uptown professional life, I got the message yet again: Appearance mattered. It meant different things in different contexts, but it mattered. More importantly, it mattered in absolutely every context.

When I now look back at the photos of me with my below-the-ear-haircut, I cringe. I look god-awful! My first reaction is "why didn't anybody tell me?" Well, they did . . .

IT'S ABOUT APPEARANCE—OR IS IT?

Body Power defines the social power I have based on my physical appearance and my health, or to be more precise, the perception of my health. Anybody who minimizes the importance of this power lives in a state of major denial. My personal choices may be in full harmony with, or deliberate rebellion against, the Madison Avenue standards of health and beauty. It doesn't matter, really—wherever I fall on the spectrum of social conformity, the decisions I make about how I present myself and tend to my body will enhance or diminish this power.

Have you ever watched the TV show *What Not to Wear* on TLC? Each week, hosts Stacy London and Clinton Kelly take an unsuspecting contestant, gift the person with a $5000 shopping spree, and let her loose in Manhattan's Soho for a couple of days of shopping. While she (and the occasional "he") shops for a new wardrobe, she has to follow Stacy and Clinton's style rules, personalized for each contestant to highlight her physical attributes and desired social image. This culminates in a hair-and-makeup revamp, and then the contestant returns to her hometown to face the friends who "volunteered" her for this makeover.

Cheesy as this all sounds, the personal rewards for each contestant instantly transcend the simple notion of looking better. This is not a plastic surgery show. Contestants still have the same less-than-perfect bodies they had before, they simply display them differently. Yet each subject, down-the-line, seems filled with a profound new sense of confidence after the make-over. This confidence triggers a fresh exuberance for life. And this exuberance is palpable for everyone who meets them. Contestants reclaim the body power they had lost or never known!

That's the inside job of Body Power. It transcends how attractive I am, how my body is shaped, or how healthy I am. It is in good measure about how attractive I *feel*, how healthy I *feel*, and how I *feel* about the shape of my body. It's about the relationship I have with my body.

IT'S ABOUT HEALTH—OR IS IT?

Body Power gets a lot more complicated when we experience fluctuations in our health or any of our physical ability. When I was diagnosed with HIV in the late '80s, my first physician told me I had a couple of years left to live. My body felt fine but, yes, friends were dying all around me. Much of my time during the first years after this diagnosis was taken up with tending to my body. Getting frequent tests for my vital signs, experimenting with alternative treatments, changing my eating habits, devouring literature on the mind-body connection. None of this was visible to others. I felt physically strong and wasn't in any way sick, but boy, I sure felt fragile and vulnerable when it came to my body. True Body Power was not so easy to come by!

My relationship to my body began to change yet again a few years ago, when I entered my fifties. Suddenly, I seemed to experience every symptom that "older men" get. I had to urinate more often—frequently enough that I have to take medication to curb it. I now sit only in aisle seats when I fly because I know multiple trips to the lavatory are de rigueur. I write these words the week after I found out that I have cataracts in both eyes and will need to have eye surgery. All of this, I am learning, is pretty standard stuff for a man my age. But in those three days after I saw my optometrist because the sight in one eye was rapidly deteriorating, and right before a whole menu of new tests was conducted by a cataract specialist, I felt vulnerable. Very vulnerable. What goes on in my body affects all of me—mind, soul, spirit. And this can make it pretty tough to show up in my world with full confidence!

Irony is, I have had a physical trainer for the last few years and am more fit than I have ever been. I feel more attractive than I did when I was in my twenties or thirties. But I got the message loud and clear when I first had to come to terms with my HIV diagnosis: It's not about how great I look. It's about the process of constantly re-examining the relationship to my body and adjusting to my "new normal."

When I think of the "new normal" I think of Stephen Kuusistu, an exquisite poet, writer, teacher. Stephen wrote the best-selling memoir *Planet of the Blind* about his experience of losing his eye sight. Stephen and I first met in the early 1990s, just when he was starting to go blind. Since then, circumstances have brought us back together at different times in our lives. The last time I saw Stephen was just a few years back, when he and I did a reading at New York City's Main Public Library on Fifth Avenue. Stephen now travels everywhere with Corky, his seeing-eye dog. What I remember most about that day, however, is the moment Stephen rose from his chair in the lobby outside the library's South Court Auditorium to great me. Stephen gave me a hug—a long, sustained bear hug. I felt his body as he embraced me, and it felt strong, powerful, rich with energy. It was the hug of a man who was brimming with vitality. Stephen's hug that afternoon reminded me yet again of just how much Body Power truly is an "inside job!"

IT'S ABOUT BEING COMFORTABLE IN OUR OWN SKIN, ISN'T IT?

One of my tougher coaching assignments involved working with the Senior Leadership Team of a manufacturing firm that was being divested by its parent company. As part of the divestiture process, the Leadership Team had to give presentations to companies that might potentially acquire them. The team had to sell itself even though it did not wish to be sold. Rough.

We tweaked the Powerpoint presentation and sharpened the company story the team would tell. All seemed to go well until the conversation turned to a debate over the dress code for the upcoming presentations. Sports coat or no sports coat? Within seconds a vehement argument erupted. "I will not wear a sports coat!" "This is not what we wear at work". "That is not who I am." "I have to be myself, I will not be fake!" Voices were raised, folks got out of their seat. Wow, it got hot!

I was stunned by this display of verbal fireworks over a sports coat—but then I got it. The sports coat may have been the symbol that uncorked simmering tensions within the group, but this heated exchange made me think of a phrase I often hear when I first interview a new coaching client. Before we engage in any sort of coaching, I ask my coachee a lot of questions to help us uncover potential coaching goals. In this initial chat, we chase down many different conversational alleys. At some point during this conversation, my coaching partner is likely to turn to me and simply say: "You know what, I just want to feel comfortable in my own skin!"

It's about image. It's about the body. And yes, it's about how we feel inside of it. No wonder that taking a look at our Body Power can evoke a lot of emotions!

FIVE WAYS TO BETTER PLUG INTO YOUR BODY POWER

Here are some concrete ways in which you can enhance your Body Power. They are pretty straightforward. They work only if they become habits. People with lots of Body Power have a great sense of discipline around how they maintain their health and appearance. And since we change over time and our bodies change, it is helpful to regularly examine the disciplines we have created for ourselves.

1. **Make physical fitness a true priority.**

   That means I honor my body. I find a physical routine that helps my body stay fit, and I commit to this routine. Especially in times of high stress and rigorous professional demands, I choose to not abandon my routine. I remember that when I feel good in my body, I feel good about connecting with others.

2. **Eat food that energizes you.**

   I acknowledge that my body needs fuel and can readily run out of gas. I choose to consistently fuel it with high-octane gas. I know my body well enough to know what energizes it and what depresses it. I remember that when my body is energized, my connections with people are energized.

3. **Have a personal sense of style.**

   Since appearance matters, I make choices about how I wish to appear. It's not about being a slave to fashion or creating an outlandish image (though if you fancy that, fine too!). If I am someone who tends to hide behind a wall of neutral choices, I choose to be visible instead. I have a point of view about my appearance!

4. **Listen to your body.**

   Our bodies tell us when they need rest. They tell us when they need food, when they need exercise, when they need to be cleansed. When we fight what the body needs, we diminish our ability to be fully present and engage with others "at our best." I choose to not fight my body.

5. Pay attention to how you feel about your body.

You may be in love with your body. You may be in despair over the flaws you see. Notice these feelings—they tend to support or hinder the way you show up in the world. Anything short of true acceptance will always diminish our body power. I will change what I don't like or choose to accept it.

VI. CHARISMA POWER

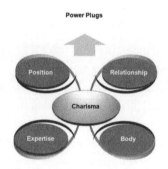

The notion of charisma makes grown men and women tremble. It brings us face-to-face with the one thing we believe we can't acquire—our big looming deficit in the successful connection game, if you will. It terrifies the self-proclaimed introvert who equates it with extroversion. It points to the one deep inner flaw of the alpha male and alpha female, the trait that all of their social skill and drive cannot will into existence.

Or so we think.

I place charisma smack in the middle of the power plugs because—well, I believe that folks who have it are blessed with a striking social advantage. Since all power plugs are interconnected, let's take a moment to extricate charisma from the other powers. Beauty ultimately rests in the eye of the beholder, and there are plenty of beautiful people who entirely lack charisma. There are many folks in high social positions with no charisma whatsoever. There are lots of folks with great subject-matter knowledge who can bore the heck out of us; if you have ever attended an academic conference, you know! Can we have relationship power without having charisma? Absolutely, although I believe that charisma instantly enhances our ability to draw people to us and hold their attention.

What exactly is charisma? The roots of the word "charisma" hail back to ancient Greek.

The term **charisma** (pl. *charismata, adj. charismatic*) has two denotations: 1) a compelling attractiveness or charm that can inspire devotion in others, 2) a divinely conferred power or talent.[8]

In the modern etymology of fame and celebrity, folks with charisma are often described as having the "it" factor. John Potts, the author of the wonderfully meticulous *A History of Charisma*, offers his own easily digestible take on the word: "The contemporary meaning of charisma is broadly understood as a special innate quality that sets certain individuals apart and draws others to them."[9]

Innate quality. We're back to the notion that "you either have it or you don't," aren't we? In an illuminating essay in the *New York Times* titled "A gift from the Musical Gods," Zachary Woolfe dissects the presence of charisma in opera performers. He, too, comes down on the side of "if you don't have it, you'll never get it." Woolfe names a legion of great opera singers who are technically skilled, enjoy exceptional careers, but lack the "it" factor. He offers Maria Callas, one of the great iconic opera divas, as an example of a singer who by most people's accounts oozed charisma:

"Her conception of the role," New York Times critic Harold Schonberg wrote about her triumphant return to the Met in 1965 in the role of Tosca, after a seven year absence, "was electrical." As if to drive home the point, he added that "the stage presence shown by Callas in her performance would have raised the hackles on a deaf man."[10]

CHARISMA AND SEX

The use of the word "electrical" to describe the impact of Maria Callas tickles my fancy. That's where I see a glimmer of hope for all of us whose charisma fuse wasn't pre-wired by the gods. It's impossible for me to contemplate charisma without thinking of the sort of energy a person emits. I thank psychologist Dr. Margarita Gurri for her strong point of view on this matter. Margarita firmly insisted I use the word "charisma" in our power plugs model. Margarita is one of those folks who many colleagues and friends will describe as charismatic. Her presence immediately lights up any room. Her energy is bold and fearless. Her sense of playfulness is, yes, infectious!

Old-school Freudian that she is, Margarita's fervor about the word "charisma" is rooted in her belief that everything ultimately comes down to sex and sexual energy. This makes her a very fun conversationalist—any conversation with Margarita quickly devolves into sexual innuendo! Like Margarita, I believe that charisma is our connection to, and expression of, a primal energy. Animal energy, sexual energy, spiritual energy. These words encompass the mythological qualities of personal charisma. I also view charisma as a force; the terms "life force" or "force of nature" come to mind. That's as far as I will go in codifying what cannot be codified. We will mine this terminology in more detail when we explore the fourth level of connection—the Energy Level!

This is the perspective I find most helpful as a coach: I view charisma, in its simplest form, as an expression of primal energy. If charisma is essentially primal energy, I know that I will be able to access it, because I have this energy. We all have it. I may not know what it feels like. I may not feel connected to it. I may not have been born with my channel to this energy wide open; I may have, in fact, been socialized to keep the channel tightly shut. But it is already here, and I simply need to find my way to it.

FLIP THE QUESTION

So the question, for me, no longer is whether I have it or not. The question is whether I can find a way to access that which is, to use Mr. Pott's phrase, "innately there."

I invite you to refrain from quantifying your charisma. I strongly urge you to not compare your charisma to that of others. It need not look like the charisma of Maria Callas. It may not be the big booming energy that sweeps everyone around you off their feet. It may be the quietly powerful energy that comes from the still center within you. The one benchmark I have for charisma, regardless of how it manifests, is this: A person with charisma generates a kinetic reaction in us. We have this reaction because of her physical radiance, the power of her ideas, the animated-ness of her personal expression, and the commitment she has to being boldly and fully present with us, in that moment! Now, that doesn't sound all that daunting any more, does it?

FIVE WAYS TO BETTER PLUG INTO YOUR CHARISMA POWER

Take a look at the following five tips for releasing your charisma power. I think of them as little baby steps toward beginning to unlock charisma that may be dormant and just waiting to bust out!

1. Enjoy being the center of attention.

It's a simple decision that immediately challenges you to show up more fully. And the moment you do, unexpected forces within you will suddenly be unleashed!

2. Put fire into the conversation.

When you feel strongly about an idea, an anecdote, a point of view, put fire into how you express it. Raise your voice, emphasize words, let your body punctuate what you say. Unexpected forces within you will be unleashed!

3. Express an impulse.

When you sense a burst of energy, a rush of heat, a dash of excitement as you speak—don't shut it down. Ride the wave. Unexpected forces within you will be unleashed!

4. Choose visceral language.

Language contains energy. Since a charismatic connection is a visceral connection, choose language that is visceral. "Brilliant." "Dazzling." "Pungent." "Sizzling." "Wrenching." "Brimming." The list is endless. When you speak visceral words, you connect with the visceral part of you. Unexpected forces within you will be unleashed!

5. Think 20%.

Show us 20% more of you. 20% more of everything we just reviewed in tips 1–4. Don't try to figure out how to do it, just think "20% more" and take a leap of faith. You may not know the "20% more of you person," but chances are, it's a more charismatic person. Unexpected forces within you will become unleashed!

VII. PLAY THE 5 X 5!

We just took a peek at how to best tap into our power plugs, and how doing so will help us to create a deeper connection with another person. Just as crucial, of course, is our ability to under-stand how our conversation partner derives her sense of power. Which of her power plugs does she value? How richly rewarding it is when we engage well with her sources of her personal power! We are now truly dipping into everything that makes both of us compelling, intriguing, engaged individuals.

How do we know what power plugs matter to another per-son? Well, if we have been around someone for a while we likely have a pretty good idea. We may not have thought of them as power plugs, but we know. A power plug is a strong source of the individual's identity—the values that define him, the pas-sions that drive him, the quirks that set him apart from the next person.

When you meet someone for the first time, throw out a question or two. Test what resonates with the other person. Most folks tell us very quickly, directly or indirectly, what makes them tick. Notice when the face gets animated, the voice gets louder, the body starts to lean toward you, the answers get elaborate, the stories start to flow. Yep, you have tapped one of their power plugs!

I call this section my 5 x 5: Five Tips for Five Power Plugs. Since most folks are powered by more than one of the plugs, this gives us lots of fuel for engaging with them. As you read the 5x5, I hope you will have a few "aha, yes, I already do that" moments. Great. Those insights are just as critical as the discovery of new tips. "Aha, yes, I do that" is an invitation to keep doing it!

I urge you to focus especially on those power plugs that may make you a little uncomfortable. Do you tend to shrivel around folks with a lot of position power? Do you want to run from folks with lots of charisma? Do folks with lots of body power make you feel inadequate? If any of the power plugs create a bit of discomfort in you, chances are you will discover some ways to "play better" with them!

I. PLAYING WELL WITH POSITION POWER—WHEN THE OTHER PERSON HAS A GOOD DEAL OF POSITION POWER AND VALUES THIS POWER!

1. Follow Power Etiquette.

Allow the person to take the lead in the conversation. Let him have the final word. Allow him to set the conversational themes. It's a simple matter of etiquette, and an indirect way of deferring to his position power.

2. Explicitly Acknowledge the Person's Position Power.

Use phrases that explicitly refer to the person's position power:

That must have been a really tough decision to make!

What do you enjoy most about leading a global management team?

3. Indicate a Desire to Learn from the Person.

What has been the most important thing you learned in your role as a CEO?

What was it like when you had to come up with a completely new strategy overnight?

What words of wisdom might you have for me about . . . ?

4. Surprise them with an Unexpected Question.

Folks tend to play it safe when speaking to someone who has lots of position power. Don't. Take a risk and ask a surprising question—you will be remembered!

5. Don't Disappear.

It's easy to cede an entire conversation to someone with lots of position power. Stay in the conversation. Match the amount of time he takes up in the conversation.

Beware: Some folks go to the opposite extreme when faced with position power. They begin to chatter ceaselessly and start to hijack the conversation. That's never a good idea!

II. PLAYING WELL WITH RELATIONSHIP POWER—WHEN THE
OTHER PERSON HAS A GOOD DEAL OF RELATIONSHIP POWER
AND VALUES THIS POWER!

1. Acknowledge that the Person Is a Social Animal.

It's wonderful that you know so many people.
You have such a great way with people. I really admire that.

As part of this acknowledgment, let the other person
know how much you enjoy speaking with her:

It's such a treat to speak with you.
I always feel stimulated by our conversations.

2. Ask for Social Introductions.

Such a request is a total win-win. You celebrate the relationship power of your friend and get to meet someone else
you have wanted to meet!

Better yet, the act of a social introduction deepens the
connection between you and the friend who makes the
introduction for you.

3. Choose Stories.

Your conversation partner will likely do this freely, anyway—but convey even more interest by eliciting a story or
two from him.

Folks who tell stories like hearing stories, in turn. Your
story will resonate best if it matches themes you picked up
in your conversation partner's story. The golden rule: Match
his themes, don't try to better his story!

4. Suggest a Follow-Up.

Someone who thrives on relationship connections will
appreciate your interest in following up on the conversation
you're having.

Suggest only follow-up activities that sincerely interest you. Best are activities that are motivated by a genuine

curiosity in the other person rather than an ulterior motive. And then, by all means, follow-up!

5. Use Lots of "We" Language.

"I" language is great for stating my point of view. "We" language indicates my appreciation of shared experiences with other people.

Folks who thrive on Relationship Power appreciate "we" talk. It stresses the existing or emerging bond between you; it indicates your desire to be "in relationship" with the person.

III. PLAYING WELL WITH KNOWLEDGE POWER — WHEN THE OTHER PERSON HAS A GOOD DEAL OF KNOWLEDGE POWER AND VALUES THIS POWER!

1. Inquire about Their Knowledge.

Some folks with lots of knowledge talk about what they know at the drop of a hat. Many, however, censor themselves greatly, especially when they talk to someone who does not share the same area of expertise.

Ask questions about the person's realm of knowledge. Your question gives her permission to open wide her knowledge door.

2. Seek Clarification.

Do not fake knowledge when you don't have knowledge. Asking for clarification with a person who has lots of knowledge power is a wonderful way of honoring that knowledge. And you will learn something you didn't know before!

3. Ask for Advice.

If someone has more knowledge and expertise in an area than you do, please ask the person for guidance. It's another great way of acknowledging that expertise. People love to be asked for help—and they love to help!

Inquiring about a lesson your conversation partner has learned is an indirect way of inviting advice. You are encouraging him to share some very personal points of view. And we know by now that a point of view always propels a conversation forward.

4. Match/Contrast Knowledge with Knowledge.

When we match knowledge, we listen to our conversation partner's knowledge and match it with knowledge from our area of expertise.

Interesting! The process an actor follows when he prepares for a role is in some ways very similar to the way an engineer creates a project map.

When we contrast knowledge with knowledge, we highlight approaches from our area of expertise that are decidedly different from the approaches that our conversation partner has shared:

Interesting! So this is what you were taught as engineers. Here's a very different outlook that we were taught in acting school!

Matching and contrasting work best when they are conveyed in a spirit of curiosity rather than one-upmanship!

5. Uncover the Origins.

Especially with folks who care deeply about what they do and excel at their work, return to our curiosity questions. They will open magical doors for you.

Why did you decide to become a biochemist?
When did you know that you wanted to become a police officer?
What drew you to landscape design?

IV. PLAYING WELL WITH BODY POWER — WHEN THE OTHER PERSON HAS A GOOD DEAL OF BODY POWER AND VALUES THIS POWER!

1. Offer a Compliment.

Compliment their appearance, their fitness, their sense of style. This may seem terribly obvious, but we do not do this often enough.

Make sure the compliment is heartfelt and specific. "Gee, you look great today!" is pleasant. "I couldn't help but notice how your smile looks absolutely radiant today" is better!

2. Talk about Being "in" the Body.

Folks who value physical health and vitality tend to be very in tune with their bodies. They acutely experience their bodily sensations—aches, adrenaline rushes, energy fluctuations, changes in their bodily functions.

In turn, talk about how your body feels, what you do to make your body feel strong, an extraordinary sensation you may have in your body. This will resonate with a body-powered person.

3. Talk about Self-Care.

Folks who value body power tend to like exercise, sports, nutrition, and a high level of self-discipline. Open the door to a chat about personal routines that they value, and you will be richly rewarded.

4. Excavate their Senses.

Folks who value appearance and physical strength tend to view the world through a sensual lens. They appreciate beauty, they like to feel good, they enjoy physical sensations. Refer to the five senses as you speak, and you will advance the conversation.

5. Hold your Own.

No matter how "cool" we think we are, it is easy to shrivel around folks with impressive body power. In spite of ourselves, we may become silent. We may find ourselves secretly resentful.

We may be comparing ourselves to the person. We may avoid the body power folks altogether. Notice your own reactions in the face of body power. Switch to a conversational track that allows you to connect with the person behind the body power.

V. PLAYING WELL WITH CHARISMA POWER—WHEN THE OTHER PERSON HAS A GOOD DEAL OF CHARISMA AND VALUES THIS CHARISMA!

1. Respect the Charisma.

Folks with lots of charisma are used to getting attention and getting it easily. Give them the attention they're used to. Allow yourself to be seduced, charmed, and inspired by them. Don't fight it!

2. Tap into Your Own Charisma.

Though you may believe you're not a charismatic person, take steps towards discovering your own unique charisma. This will be especially helpful when you engage with a charismatic personality. Review the Charisma tips in the preceding section.

3. Match Their Energy.

Experiment with matching the energy of a charismatic person, even if you don't believe "that's you." It may pull you out of your comfort zone—and pull amazing things from inside of you!

4. Speak Their Language.

Charismatic folks tend to revel in language. Revel in language with them. Revel in the language that they seem to enjoy. It's a great short-cut to a deeper connection. Remember—language is an aphrodisiac.

5. Be Fearless.

Charismatic folks also tend to be less fearful than others. It's not that they don't know fear—they just do a better job of overriding fear with the sheer force of their personality. Consider, for a moment, overriding your social fears as well. Act as if they weren't there, and see what happens!

SUMMARY

Our second level of connection is the Power Level. When we connect well with our own sources of power, we connect more richly with another person. When we don't, we are actively interfering with our social engagement at the Talk Level. And the moment we begin to deliberately play well with the power sources of another person, we truly accelerate the connection with that individual.

To help us enhance something as elusive as a sense of personal power, we consider five sources of this power: Our professional or social position. Our relationships. Our expertise. Our body. And our charisma.

We use the notion of a "power plug" to describe these sources. Just as we light up a dark room by plugging into a light source, the word "plug" suggests that a personal source of power is available to us. It also implies that we need to consciously connect with it. Yes, we need to plug in!

YOUR FIVE-STEP GUIDE TO CONNECTING WELL AT THIS LEVEL

I. Take a quick test—your personal Power Plugs Barometer. Discover which of your plugs are burning hot and which may be arctic cold.
II. Read up on the five power plugs. Notice the information that most resonates with you. Your reactions as you read this chapter will guide you to where you can better plug in.
III. Look at the specific suggestions for better plugging into your power plugs—you will find them at the end of each individual power plug section. Consider the tips that you're willing to "test" as you engage with folks.

IV. Review the suggestions for better playing with the power plugs of others. Consider the tips you're willing to "test" here, as well.

V. Put the tips you selected into action. Even two or three new behaviors will immediately change how you connect at the Power Level. Enjoy—you're beginning to dance in the invisible world!

Chapter 4

Level Three: Intent Charges the Atmosphere

Four Levels of Connection

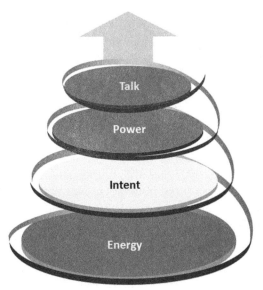

Table Five: Our third level of connection

We create what we think. Right?

I realize that not everyone who is reading this statement will ascribe to its sentiment. Since this notion is at the core of our third level, here's a quick history lesson on the origins of this—well, line of thinking.

Travel back with me to a time between the World Wars. Three entirely different developments unfolded around parallel lines. The New Thought movement began to reach a tipping point in the United States. Charles Fillmore, the Founder of Unity Church and a prominent figure among New Thought leaders, had gathered his first congregation in Kansas City well before the advent of World War I, but his churches and their message truly proliferated between the wars. Ernest Holmes, the founder of Religious Science of Mind, rose to prominence in the late 1920s and quickly established an impassioned following. Norman Vincent Peale's book *The Power of Positive Thinking* wasn't published until 1952, but Peale and comrades like Dale Carnegie had been preaching the positive-thought message since the 1930s.

These voices were not homogeneous. The first two gentlemen champion an explicitly spiritual world view that links every human being to the concept of an all-pervasive universal mind. The latter two emphasize the importance of simple, positive action that propels life forward in a positive way. The thread that connects all four of them, however, is a very simple belief: *What we think defines the reality that unfolds. Positive forecasting manifests a more desirable reality.*

Does this sound too simplistic? You say you want proof? Well, a second movement entered public consciousness around the very same time: quantum physics. In 1905 Einstein forever changed the way we look at reality with $E = mc^2$. Atoms, according to Einstein, could be broken down into subatomic particles such as quarks and photons. These subatomic particles were pure energy. Put simply and stripped down to its essentials, everything, and absolutely everything, is energy. While Einstein believed that this energy had a solid form, Thomas Young's wave theory of light had postulated that matter existed in the form of waves and was not solid at all.

Think of Niels Bohr, the Nobel-prize winning contemporary of Einstein, as the mediator between these seemingly irreconcilable views on how energy manifests. Bohr believed that energy could exist in both wave form and particles. More specifically, he was certain that subatomic particles consisted of waves which then turned into particles. In 1927, the now-famous "Copenhagen Interpretation" cemented this perspective into a game-changing remix of the cause-and-effect relationship between energy and matter: Subatomic particles, when studied in their wave form, will be perceived in either wave form or matter based on the individual thought of the scientist who is observing them. Put simply, the thoughts and beliefs of the individual determine the manner in which energy shows up.

Decades later, everything that is said in the human potential field still harks back to Niels Bohr and the Copenhagen findings. *What I think determines the way my physical reality unfolds.* It is so simple and so bold. It still sounds utterly radical, after all these years.

SO WHAT DOES ACTING HAVE TO DO WITH IT?

Here's our third track—and since I began my professional life coaching actors, this one is especially dear to my heart. While Albert Einstein and New Thought teachers were turning our understanding of reality upside down, Konstantin Stanislavksy, a Russian theatre director, forever changed the way actors act. Why the heck does that matter, you may wonder? After all, theatre and film exist primarily to entertain and enlighten us! Indeed. Actors, however, have to inhabit their characters, and the skills they employ to create a compelling stage relationship uncannily mirror the skills we use in "real life" to engage with another person.

Before Stanislavsky, acting tended to look like one big, melodramatic version of reality. Heightened emotions, larger-than-life gestures. Nowadays we expect an actor to portray a believable version of reality when he portrays a role. This way of representing reality was formulated and refined by Stanislavsky in the 1920s and 30s. He invented the tools of sense memory and physical action as a way of helping an actor to connect with the humanity of a character. And—drumroll now—Stanislavsky insisted that, scene-by-scene, an actor play his character's objective. Objective is actor-speak for having a clear intent. And the singular assumption behind playing the objective is this: The moment I have a clear objective in mind, a scene will unfold more powerfully. My thought will both define and magnify the impact I have on the other character. It will crystallize my stage relationship.

Can it be? Yes—The New Thought Movement, Niels Bohr, Konstantin Stanislavsky, they are all affirming the very same principle. Say it three times over. *Thought determines how reality unfolds. Thought determines how reality unfolds. Thought determines how reality unfolds.*

It's great fun to contemplate our life's goals and dreams—I call those the big intentions. But in this chapter, we will look at how our clear and conscious intent will shape the simple, everyday conversation. The little moments that yield mega-rewards.

OUR THREE CORE INTENTS

In the pages that follow, we will examine three different aspects of intent as we embrace our third level of connection:

> **Core Intent #1:** I create the impact I desire.
>
> **Core Intent #2:** I create the tone I desire.
>
> **Core Intent #3:** I choose the social roles I will play.

Regardless of which of these intents I contemplate, the moment I get clear about my intent I bring a higher degree of purpose to any encounter. My intent forces me to be present. I cannot run on automatic pilot since my thoughts are actively helping to shape the encounter with someone else. Let us be very explicit about one thing: Intent is not mind control. Intent does not imply that I try to force the flow or outcome of a conversation. I cannot ultimately control the behavior of another person, and I cannot will something into existence for which the moment isn't right. My clarity of intent merely contributes to the unfolding of the conversation. That it does brilliantly!

Students of "intention thinking" sometimes get frustrated when their intentions don't manifest. You may be familiar with that line of reasoning—hey, I have summoned a powerful thought, so why doesn't the intent of my thought magically unfold right here and now? Well, there are a myriad of reasons. When we look at how we relate to others, intent is—pardon the pun—intentionally the third level of our Four Levels, not the first. For intent to have impact, it needs to be supported by skill at the Talk Level and an ability to play well at the Power Level. Without a basic measure of competence at the first two levels, every intent is instantly hampered by our public behavior. While we are thinking the thought, we're at once running active interference with the intent of this thought!

CORE INTENT #1: CREATE THE IMPACT YOU DESIRE

We can learn a lot from actors. Take a look at the work of two of my favorites, Susan Sarandon and Sean Penn. I suggest Susan Sarandon in *The Client* and Sean Penn in *Milk*. And I suggest Sarandon and Penn together in *Dead Man Walking*. All four are Oscar-nominated performances, deservedly so. Sarandon won for *Dead Man*, Penn for *Milk*. Frame by frame, their performances are sharp, crisp, luminous.

Penn and Sarandon are smart actors. They dig deep emotionally, but they never splatter the character's emotions all over the screen. Instead of "playing the emotion," they "play the objective." This gives their performances focus and direction. That's what I love when I watch their work: I see clear intent in action, right there on the screen. Simply marvelous.

Here's one thing every actor learns at some point in acting class: You take a scene in a script and you break it into beats. A beat usually describes one clear line of action in the script, a through-line if you will. We know that a beat ends and a new beat begins when there is a major shift or change in the conversation. Within each beat the actor, of course, speaks the lines from the script. More importantly, though, the actor picks an objective for the beat. The objective is the actor's secret little mantra, if you will. It is never stated out loud but it is vivid in the actor's mind. Actors know that the moment they find a clear objective for a beat, it gives everything they say a strong purpose. It charges the words with energy. It lifts the scene to a higher level of intensity. There are three golden rules that actors know about an objective:

1. The objective needs to be an action verb.
2. It needs to describe the impact I seek to have on another person.
3. It needs to be visceral for me.

Action verbs matter because they unleash forward-moving velocity. They propel us toward the other person. More important, however, is this: An objective needs to be "a turn-on" in the brain. Actors love to do synonym searches to find the objectives that really get their juices flowing. My objective in a scene might be to "excite you." Fine—but what if, instead, it were to "agitate you," to "incite you," to "impassion you," to "titillate you?" There is no such thing as a right or wrong objective, but there are not-so-good objectives. Good objectives stimulate my brain, strike my fancy, spark my imagination.

So—let's take this very simple notion and apply it to our everyday relating.

CREATING INTENT IN FORMAL PRESENTATIONS

Not every moment in a professional relationship needs to produce Oscar-worthy fireworks. But I see it over and over again in my work as a coach: Just as a clear objective illumines any stage relationship, clear intent has the potential to illumine any professional or personal relationship. When I clarify my intent, the relationship will change—yes, must change—because my intent toward the other person has changed. And the beauty of intent? It is simple. It is invisible. It costs nothing. It is a thought that is available to me at all times. I simply need to choose it.

Three principles will help you to select an intent that works for you. These principles entirely match the guidelines we just reviewed:

Three Intent Principles

1. Pick an action verb.
2. The verb needs to describe the impact you wish to have on another person.
3. Pick a verb that stimulates the heck out of you!

The power of our intent resides in the crispness of our thought. "I kinda, sorta would like to make a good impression on you" won't do it. "I want to dazzle you" may! If the verb "dazzle" doesn't click with you, no problem. Find a verb that does. Vague and rambling intents will create vague and rambling conversations. Crisp intents electrify a conversation!

If you ever took an oral interpretation or public speaking class in college, your professor likely asked you to play with different types of intent. Great. Intent is especially crucial in any public speaking situation. In a business meeting we don't just get up and stand in front of a group of people to babble about something or other. We usually have a certain amount of time in which we are the center of attention, and during this time we're expected to make an impact. Clear intent helps us do just that. Here are some "classic" intents that can be helpful when we speak in public:

Sample Intents:

- To motivate you
- To persuade you

- To inspire you
- To entertain you
- To move you
- To challenge you
- To enchant you
- To provoke you
- To delight you

Just as in acting, it is possible to have multiple intents in a single presentation. Not at the same time, please—that will create one big "kinda, sorta" muddle. But there can be a section in which I seek to move my audience, another one in which I challenge the audience, a third in which I inspire it. The beauty of working with such sequential intents: I begin to enrich my presentation with a layered texture and wider palette. Each beat now has a distinctly different purpose. And just like a well-trained actor, I suddenly begin to display a broader personal range. This range sharpens the impact I have on folks in ways I cannot possibly know!

CREATING INTENT IN INFORMAL CONVERSATIONS

Clear intent is equally potent in a one-on-one conversation. The more formal the purpose for our conversation, the more attuned we tend to be to the notion of intent. In a job interview, for example, our intent may be to impress the interviewer. In a sales situation, our intent may be to outsmart the seller. If we are the salesperson, our intent may be to motivate the other person toward a quick purchase. When we go on a date, our intent may be to charm the person we're dating. These are intuitive intents. We may not focus on them with great rigor, but they are part and parcel of the social narrative of the situation. If we violate this narrative, we will likely confuse the heck out of the other person. If we get lucky this may work in our favor; more often than not, it won't!

Think of all the other situations in which we chat with a person and just carry on about something or other and "kill time." That's the bulk of our conversations, isn't it? At times, such conversations can be a delicious diversion and exactly what we desire, with that individual, in that moment. No intent needed. What if we, however, approached each of those situations with conscious intent, as well?

Consider, for example, a moment when you grab a bite with a colleague in the cafeteria. You may habitually chat about incidents that happened at work, a current news topic, the outcome of a sports game. Watercooler stuff. What if the next time you hang out with the same colleague, you experiment with deliberate intent? What if the intent were "to surprise," "to amuse," "to stimulate," "to startle," "to astound" your colleague? You get to pick the intent. Have fun with it. Your intent will challenge you to use fresh language, tell new stories, ask unexpected questions. Try the same approach at a cocktail reception, a networking event. Notice how much more purposeful even a quick throwaway conversation suddenly becomes. Revel in the surprises that are sure to unfold!

"CREATE IMPACT" INTENT EXERCISE

Here's a simple exercise you may wish to conduct with a group of friends or colleagues. I include it in many of my workshops. It's quite powerful:

1. Gather with your group.
2. Agree on a list of six to eight intents you will use for this experiment. The "Sample Intents" list in this chapter works beautifully, or create a list of your own.
3. Select a few simple topics. Since this is an exercise about speaking with intent, select "easy" topics. Topics that tend to work well: Speak about a favorite hobby, a place in the world that you love, a cause that is dear to you, a personal belief or value that you hold in high regard.

4. Speak for 2-3 minutes on the topic of your choice.

5. Here's the important part: Before you speak, select one of the intents your group agreed on. Let this intent guide you as you speak. Keep it upfront in your mind. Do not disclose this intent to your friends before you speak, and do not utter the intent word while you talk. Remember—intent is your secret mental guide and only known to you!

6. When you are finished speaking, ask your friends to identify the intent that you used as your guide.

7. If they identify it correctly—great, you are having the impact you wish to have!

8. If your friends are unable to correctly identify your intent, ask for feedback on how you may better convey this intent. Do you need to speak with more enthusiasm? Do you need to use stronger emotional cue words? Do you need to add a compelling personal story? Do you need to linger more and rush less? Do you need to be more emphatic with key words?

Feedback on our intent is a potent tool for calibrating how other people experience us. Seek it out. Use it. If we consistently don't have the impact we wish to have, we are likely not connecting with folks as deeply as we would like. But when we adjust our external behavior so it fully matches our intent—wow, beware. Doors small and large will start to open in absolutely every conversation!

CORE INTENT #2: CREATE THE TONE YOU DESIRE

Still wondering if intent really matters?

Here's another exercise I once led in a communication skills workshop: A group of folks sit in a circle. Each person delivers a conversational phrase from a worksheet. A simple phrase like "Did you have fun at the party?" or "You look great today!" Folks have two options—they may deliver their phrase sincerely or sarcastically. We go around the circle, and each person delivers her or his phrase.

Guess what—50% of the time we could not tell if the person was intending to be sincere or sarcastic. Houston—we have a major problem here (that's sarcasm, by the way . . .)!

My tone has the power to inform the tone of an entire conversation. More significantly, my intent for the tone of a conversation will help to create that very conversation. By tone I mean the emotional timbre, the conversational texture, the affective quality, the "vibe," the "feel" of a chat. Pick the synonym that most makes sense to you. Sometimes a social context invites a specific tone. A joyous party hopefully invites a different tone than a bereavement ceremony. But more often than not, my deliberate intent will invoke the very tone that I am intending.

How do we quantify conversational tone? The moment I give a tone its name, it's easier to pinpoint exactly what it is and what it isn't. I find it helpful to think of conversational tone in terms of polar ranges. Here are some common polarities:

Tonal Polarities

Sincere	Sarcastic
Warm	Cool
Brainy	Silly
Neutral	Opinionated
Passionate	Dispassionate
Kind	Harsh
Relaxed	Tense
Playful	Serious

As you look at these polar ranges, consider the following questions:

1. Which sorts of conversations do I most often find myself in?
2. Do these conversations reflect the tonal qualities I enjoy best?
3. To what degree do I contribute to the tone of these conversations?
4. What different sort of intents might I wish to deploy to invite different conversational tones?

And yes, these questions bring us right back to our personal range, don't they? My conversation partner contributes in good measure to the tone of a conversation, but how can I become a shaper of tone instead of a victim of the other person's tone? I send you back to the skills in our Talk Level: Reframing is not only a terrific way of shifting the content of a conversation, it tends to also instantly shift its tone!

AVOID THE "SERIOUS" TRAP

Our polarities list ends with the playful/serious range. I deliberately place it last. Most formal business conversations I witness are weighted down by a somber tone that neither advances the conversation nor solves the problems folks are seeking to solve. I am especially disheartened when I watch jovial, joyous individuals turn into solemn communicators the moment they embark on a "heavy" conversation. It's as if they are sucked right into the big black hole of seriousness and don't trust their ability to infuse a different tone. I don't propose we trivialize a serious topic with a frivolous treatment. I thrive on informed debate and substantive conversations. But I also believe that we don't rescue a drowning ship by throwing more weight onto it; we help it float by unloading some of its baggage. And there are times when irreverence is the only tone that will advance a conversation!

These are two of the credos to which we aspire in my firm: "We're fun." "We drill down." It's our way of creating a frame for the tone of our trainings and our conversations. I firmly believe that a playful tone fosters engagement, commitment, and invites folks to open up. I also believe that when we drill down into the substance, knowledge, and hidden meaning of a topic, we foster curiosity and a deeper awareness. I realize that there can be an inherent tension between these two credos. We thrive on this tension. More importantly, we have learned that having fun fosters the drilling down. It helps us to do so with joy instead of arduous effort!

CORE INTENT #3: INTEND THE ROLE YOU PLAY AND PLAY IT WELL

Watch for "the split." Let me explain what I mean.

I am walking down the hallway and run into Maria. We have a breezy chat about the new change in our company's flex day policy, the firing of our VP of Sales who nobody really liked, the backup on the just-opened express lanes on I-95. I experience Maria as playful, funny, a little sarcastic maybe, and most definitely full of mischief. It's the Maria I know and appreciate, the one I look forward to chatting with, day in and day out.

Twenty minutes later, in our weekly team meeting, Maria stands up and makes a couple of logistics announcements about our upcoming team retreat. I experience Maria as a little pedantic, rather dry in her tone, and rushed. I can't wait for Maria to stop talking so I can listen to someone else.

We have all seen this sort of behavior switch, right? My brain is screaming—"What the heck happened to Maria? Where did she go?"

Now—the fact that Maria shows up differently in a new setting is terrific. The meeting is a fresh social context with different social demands. Great connectors understand the importance of the social switch. The fact that Maria shows up diminished is not terrific, at all. What I witness at the team meeting is what I call "the split." The split happens the moment I slip into a professional or social role that prevents me from showing up at my best. No, let me be more precise. The split happens because of my limiting conception of this social role. I split myself from all that is engaging, compelling, appealing, seductive, enjoyable, inspiring, stimulating about me. Worse yet—"the split" tends to happen with little or no conscious deliberation by me. I seem to suddenly follow a vaguely articulated social blueprint for how to best show up in a certain setting. And then I play the part.

Of this I'm pretty certain. Maria likely has no idea of just how diminished she is at our business meeting. She has slipped into the role of "The Professional." She has done so without any clear intent: Maria has created "the split" without wishing to do so. The narrative for the professional blueprint goes something like this: I'm efficient. I know what I'm doing and I don't make mistakes. I always follow the rules, or I sure as heck pretend I do. I play nice and will not tell you what I really think. I certainly will not show you how I feel because—well, that's not professional. I'm polished. I'm pretty darn perfect, and I will prove it to you every chance I get!

Arrgh. Let me run away from you fast. Or as Cher famously said to Nicolas Cage in *Moonstruck*: "Snap out of it!"

PLAYING TO OUR AUDIENCE

When I think of Maria, I think of sociologist Erving Goffman's *The Presentation of Self in Everyday Life*, a dazzling dissemination of the roles we don in public life. Goffman appropriates the language of dramatic structures to describe every aspect of our public performance. At one extreme, Goffman says, "we have the performer who is completely taken in by his own act; he can be sincerely convinced that the impression of reality which he stages is the real reality."[11] On the other end is the performer who is resolutely cynical about his act. Regardless of where we fall on the continuum of self-delusion and calculated detachment, there is a common thread we can never escape: The presence of an audience who observes our act.

These themes pop up unexpectedly as I hunker down at a Starbucks in Marina del Rey with my friend Irene Borger. I think of Irene as the quintessential renaissance woman. A cherished writing teacher in Los Angeles, Irene is a muse to legions of fellow writers. In her role as the director of the Alpert Award in the Arts, Irene channels the disbursement of financial awards to artistic innovators. And during her career as a journalist for major national magazines, Irene interviewed everyone from Susan Sontag and Marcel Marceau to Agnes deMille and Maurice Sendak. Irene is, above all, a master conversationalist, a quixotic spirit who slips with ease in and out of any chat.

"I need your advice on something," Irene says to me as we sip our chai tea lattes. "I am about to be interviewed for a podcast, and I'm just a little unsure of how to handle this situation. My dear colleague, Jaune Evans, is interviewing me, and even though she has sent me a list of suggested questions, it feels a little unsettling to have a conversation in front of an audience. I'm not sure of how on-message I need to be. And I don't know how much my knowledge that we're being recorded will affect how I respond, in the moment."

Irene has qualms about this podcast? I'm surprised—I figured Irene had this role thing figured out! But as we chat further I begin to understand. Irene is the one who usually inhabits the role of the interviewer. She wears it like a second skin. The role allows her to ask deliberate questions. It demands that she listen with strong intent. It has the power to uncork a wonderful level intimacy with the interviewee, an intimacy that can be especially seductive since the relationship tends to be temporary. And the role of the interviewer provides great cover. Irene gets to ask and listen; it will actually hinder her work as a journalist if she tells too much about herself.

In the upcoming podcast, a familiar role has been yanked from Irene. And yet the thing that might be most comfortable—just sitting and having a chat with Jaune—may be impacted by the presence of two audiences: The live audience that listens to the conversation in an auditorium, and the future audience that will listen to the recording.

The questions inherent in this situation are delicious. How will Jaune inhabit the role of the interviewer? How will Irene inhabit the role of the interviewee and writing expert? How will the presence of an audience, and its reaction to the flow of the conversation, impact the questions Jaune asks, the answers Irene provides, the manner in which Jaune responds to what Irene says? What sort of mental editing, deliberate or not, will be prompted by the fact that a podcast audience can later scrutinize everything that is said?

These are not academic questions. These are the sort of dilemmas we work out, one way or another, every day as we engage with folks. The chat with Irene reminds me of just how complex the layers of our public performance are. In nearly every business situation and social function, we have an audience. There is a primary audience when we make a statement in a business meeting—the folks in the room. And while what we say may not be recorded, we always have a secondary audience—all the other folks who're not in the room but may hear second-hand about a statement we made. The deeper question, then, is always this: Which self will show up when I know that others are my witness?

I have no neat answers for you. The best way I know of navigating our public performance is to do just what Irene did: By posing the question, we begin to become conscious about "our act." The way we formulate the question will ultimately clarify the choices we will make—or it will help us to surrender to all that is unanswerable.

HOW TO NOT PLAY THE ROLE

Some professional roles come with a tight set of work rules. Couple this with having an audience every moment you're in role, and it can suddenly feel like it's entirely impossible to "be yourself."

Consider this a cautionary tale. Miami is a major hub for American Airlines, and since living in South Florida, I have met quite a few folks who work for the airline. I also fly this airline once in a while—that makes me the audience. It's common knowledge that American's employees are largely disenchanted with their employer. After a series of highly contentious contract negotiations, many folks who work for AA feel like they were thrown under the bus (or the Boing 757) by management. I vividly remember several social events where I found myself chatting with groups of AA flight attendants. The same thing happened in every one of these chats: After I heard a litany of complaints about management insensitivity to flight attendant needs, excessive runway delays, mishaps in lay-over hotels and scheduling improprieties, one of the conversationalists would terminate the chat with a defiant declaration: "But no matter what happens, I will always act professional!" Everyone present would nod in equally defiant agreement. It was the one thing everyone agreed on. The flight attendant common ground.

Let's translate that statement, shall we (and I apologize in advance to every flight attendant who's not part of this narrative): I will follow all regulations when I do my job. I won't give anyone a reason to reprimand me or write me up. I will pretend that I like what I'm doing though I really don't. I will not do anything beyond what I absolutely have to do. I certainly will not be joyous while I engage with you. I will wear the mask of the consummate professional which hides my extreme displeasure at having to talk to you, right now. I will give you absolutely nothing, zilch, nada of myself!

This is professional-role-hell. Run, baby, run—as far away from you as I can.

BEWARE OF STOCK SOCIAL ROLES

When we're unsure of how to inhabit a professional role, many of us slip into stock social roles. Playing these roles can be delicious fun. Over time, this act works only when we perform it with intent—and when we know how to drop the act. There are a whole slew of social roles, but at the end of the day they all fall into one of two camps: the "Like Me" roles and the "Notice Me" roles.

"Like Me" Roles

Cheerleader. People-pleaser. Joker. Seducer. Charmer. Do any of these roles look, sound, smell familiar to you?

I was raised to be the charming boy. I'm not sure I was very good at it—but I knew that it was expected of me. I understood early on in life that part of my job as the eldest son was to make my parents look good in public. It was critical to my family's public performance, and "turning on the charm" was a surefire way of doing so. I was rewarded by my parents and everyone else for being "The Charmer." And being rewarded felt darn good!

How do I know it's a social role and not simply "part of my personality?" Well, I'm pretty sure I didn't roll out of my mother's womb genetically prewired to be the charming boy. That's a skin I crawled into somewhere along the way. It took quite a few years of therapy to fully "get" how I played the role, and then a good bit more effort to shed this well-honed mask.

Thing is—being charming really works wonders in many instances. I see it around me, every day. Folks who know how to be charming get rewarded. I have, as well, embraced the role of "The Charmer" once again. I get a kick out of turning on the charm, on occasion. It tends to disarm folks. It helps me to connect with people more quickly. And it brings out my playful side. I like that. The difference now, post-self-reflection, is this: I choose the role. The role doesn't play me. And I know when it's time to let it go.

"Notice Me" Roles

Show-Off. Prankster. Debater. Life-of-the-Party. Provocateur. We know these as well, right?

My colleague Brad Myers loves the role of "The Provocateur." He crawls into it with singular abandon. His business card actually says "Brad Myers, Provocateur." There is no "split" with this role for Brad—he claims this public identity with ueber-intent. I enjoy Brad's smarts. I love his kick-ass attitude. I get a vicarious thrill out of his delight in challenging colleagues and pushing the limits of a conversation. I have also seen this role turn sour for Brad. It happens in that split-second when Brad needs to have the final word. It happens when his desire to be right makes him sound righteous. It happens when he disrespects the power of the folks he provokes. In those moments, the fun provocateur becomes the bad boy who doesn't play well with others. That role doesn't serve Brad, ever.

Here's the question Brad's fling with "The Provocateur" poses for all of us: Even when I intend my social role, do I intend the social consequences of this role? Am I able to notice when a role turns on me? I offer you the actor's answer: Inhabit your role with full commitment, and know when to leave the role behind. Don't typecast yourself and play the same role over and over again. Notice which roles foster connection, which don't. And above all, enjoy the deliberate exploration of your public self!

SUMMARY

The moment I contemplate intent, I consider the possibility of showing up with a greater sense of purpose for any conversation I have, large or small. Instead of falling victim to how a conversation unfolds, I know that a few simple choices I make will significantly influence the flow and direction of a chat. Great connectors don't just fall into conversations, they help to shape them with conscious intent. How delicious!

The beauty of intent is that it is nothing more than a thought I hold in my consciousness. It is simple. It is invisible. It costs nothing. It is available to me at all times. I simply need to choose it.

121

The moment I clarify my intent, the relationship with another person will change—yes, must change—because my intent toward that person has changed. Three core intents will have a significant impact on a conversation:

> **Core Intent #1:** My clear conscious intent creates the impact I desire.
>
> **Core Intent #2:** My clear conscious intent creates the tone I desire.
>
> **Core Intent #3:** My clear conscious intent chooses the social roles I will play.

Action verbs are our key to creating powerful intents. Action verbs unleash forward-moving velocity. They propel us toward the other person. For these action verbs to "work," they need to be crisp and truly electrify our brains.

Tonal polarities help us better understand the kind of tone we tend to infuse into our conversations, and they remind us that our intent influences the emotional texture of a conversation. It behooves us to pay special attention to the playful/serious polarity. While many business conversations tend to have a serious quality, we have the power to infuse them with a more playful tone. This accelerates the level of engagement, and the ease with which a conversation unfolds.

And we decide to watch for the "split"—the moment in any business situation when we inhabit a professional or social role without clean intent. When we step into the "split," we're following a barely articulated and limiting blueprint for how we should conduct our public performance. We split ourselves from all that is engaging, compelling, appealing, seductive, enjoyable, inspiring, stimulating about us. The one sure-fire way to avoid the "split" is to actively choose the social roles we play. We do this with intent—and we know when to drop the role!

Chapter 5

Level Four: Energy Conquers All

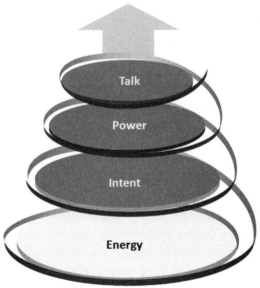

Four Levels of Connection

Talk

Power

Intent

Energy

Table 6: Our fourth level of connection

"The light is on."

I have used this phrase for years to describe folks who stimulate me. I used it without thinking much about what it actually means, or what the language I was using implied. I don't see auras, so I was not describing the perception of light fields. The light, I realize now, refers to a certain mental agility that I appreciate in people. A quick mind that likes to contemplate new ideas and possibilities. The light also refers to an openness I see in the person's face. Eyes that sparkle and beam with curiosity. More importantly, however—the light describes a certain quality of being. One of my favorite book titles of all time is Milan Kundera's *The Unbearable Lightness of Being*. I actually like the title more than I like the book itself. Yes, folks whose "light is on" emanate a sweet lightness of being. I realize that I am now venturing into abstract terrain—but when I mention lightness, I am ultimately talking about the energy that radiates from a person. And this energy encompasses everything—the quality of the thoughts, the openness of their expression, the presence of a big and generous spirit, the vibrations the person emits.

When we begin to dissect the energy experience, it is tempting to make something that is very simple overly complicated. We won't do that in *Infectious*. I have to chuckle every time I read a scientific article that disputes the existence of energy fields or questions the scientific evidence that supports their existence. What we're talking about is already part of our everyday vernacular. On some level or other, we all know it. We name it every time we say that a person has "a bad vibe" or "bad energy." We name it when we say that "there is lots of energy behind that comment." We name it when we declare that someone has an "infectious energy." The notion that infectious energy creates infectious connections is, of course, the premise of this book. We can pick this language apart all we want, but the bottom line is this: Our language pinpoints those moments when we're having a visceral reaction to a person—or to be more precise, a person's energy.

Cultures throughout history have found language to describe this energy. The most common phrase attributed to it is "life force." The Hindus call it *prana*, the Japanese *ki*, the Chinese *qi* or *chi*. There are almost 100 other names associated with this energy in as many different cultures. Breath, and the way we breathe, is by most cultures viewed as the source of this original life force. It is the same as "the light" to which I referred at the start of this chapter.

These ways of understanding energy are deeply ingrained in nearly all non-Western societies. For many centuries there was a renegade movement of Western thinkers called vitalists. Vitalists believed that beyond chemistry and biology, there was a "vital spark" or "élan vital"—two favorite vitalist terms—that were the source of all human behavior. Vitalists greatly influenced the work of many non-traditional body healers. Einstein validated the vitalists and terminated their renegade status, once and for all, when he proclaimed that everything is energy. Which brings us right back to the research of Pentland and Olguín that kicked off this book.

"It's all about energy." Period. End of discussion. Right?

Think of it this way: Here's where the real joy of connecting begins. The moment we begin to have a deeper experience of energy, we're beginning to tap the real "juice" in our relationships. "Energy" is the fourth and final level of connection. It is the realm where all connections that truly resonate unfold. I believe that as we know energy more consciously, we flow more consciously with the energy of another person. These are some of the tantalizing questions we'll explore in this chapter: How do we experience energy? How do we access it? And how do we hang out with the energy of others? You may have fantastic verbal skills. You may be in touch with your power plugs and fully load them. You may be one of those folks who always show up with clear intent. Awesome! If your energy does not resonate with others, and if the energy of others does not penetrate to you, your relationships tend to consistently fall short of true resonance. You're successful, possibly very successful—but you're likely hitting that glass ceiling of connectivity more often than you'd like.

HOW WE KNOW ENERGY

As I embarked on writing this book, I had chats with two colleagues whom I have known for a good two decades. Melanie Hahn Roche is an internationally-known energy healer with a thriving private practice in Miami and substantial experience in training other energy healers. Arnie Kolodner is a beloved children's magician in New York City with an "underground" healing practice. "So what is energy?" I asked them. The answer from both was identical: "Well, everything is!" Ah, yes. That again. But how does this answer help you and me to fully engage with others? I believe that we cannot begin to play with energy and fully receive the energy of others until we know how we experience it. I think of a marvelous ancient Sufi story that was relayed to me by Dr. Isaac Goren, a medical qi gong practitioner and teacher in South Florida:

> The Prophet Muhammad held a small jar with honey in his hand and asked a group of his disciples: "What is this?" One after another, the disciples pointed at the content of the jar and said: "Well, that's honey." The last of the disciples, however, paused. Ali then dipped a finger into the jar, scooped up a bit of the inside and licked it with his tongue. He then looked at the others and declared: "Yes, it is honey." The group looked at the Prophet Muhammad for confirmation. "Only Ali knows honey," the Prophet declared.

So, let's take a look at some of the ways in which we dip into the jar of energy, shall we? Since our experience of energy tends to be private and personal, here are some very personal stories about how some of us "taste" energy.

Let me take you to a little hole-in-the-wall restaurant in Hallandale Beach, Florida, not far from where I live. Surf Road Tacos. It was nestled in a small derelict warehouse district right off Dixie Highway. You could miss it with a blink of an eye if you didn't pay attention. When I finally stopped and stepped inside, I realized that everything about Surf Road Tacos spoke to me: the cheap California beach shack décor, the fresh, tasty, and inexpensive cali-mex treats on the menu, the eclectic clientele, the friendly multi-cultural staff. Soon I began to look forward to my almost daily jaunts to Hallandale to get my Surf Road Tacos fix.

When the owner announced that she was closing Surf Road Tacos, I felt an instant pang of sadness. Part of my routine that gave me so much pleasure would be yanked from me! This sadness got an unexpected reprieve by an eleventh hour announcement. A new owner would take over Surf Road Tacos, keep the place open, retain the name, offer the same menu. Whew. Cool!

That is, indeed, what happened. Surf Road Tacos remained open. Same décor. Same food. Same prices. And yet—Surf Road Tacos would never be the same. Most of the staff was gone, and with it, the spirit of the place. I felt it. Other customers felt it. The energy of the place had irrevocably changed. Two weeks later, Surf Road Tacos closed for good.

During a flight to Los Angeles later that month, my seat-mate and I drift into a conversation about energy. "I used to be a housing inspector," he says to me. "I have walked into thousands of houses. Don't let anybody tell you that houses don't have energy." He had impressed me as a gruff and somewhat serious fellow, and I'm surprised by his comment. I'm having one of my "don't judge a book by its cover" moments. As he speaks I flash back to sensations I have had when I was entering certain rooms. I think of all the spaces I have walked into that seemed cluttered and claustrophobic. The kind of spaces you want to flee the moment you enter them. I also think of the sort of spaces that felt expansive and airy and seemed to be brimming with light. The kind of spaces in which I want to start to dance. I'm an architect's son, and I remember the institutional architecture that my dad built. I doubt that any of those buildings were influenced by feng shui, the Chinese art of arranging spaces in a way that facilitates positive energy flow. My dad's buildings felt meticulous, cool, alienating. Yes, I am very much affected by the energy of the space I visit.

REMOVING ENERGY BLOCKS

When Melanie Hahn Roche talks about her first significant experience of energy, she also comments on how she suddenly saw and "felt" the environment around her differently.

> I went to therapy for years. I had lots of things to deal with, but therapy didn't create real changes for me. It provided me with insights—but nothing really shifted. I got a lump in my breast at the age of 32. That's when I went to see my first healer. When I left that initial session on the Upper West Side, I walked over to Riverside Park before heading to the subway. I remember on the walk to the park, all these babies in strollers kept reaching out to me as their strollers were pushed past, as if to say, 'Pick me up. Play with me.' And dogs on leashes were running up to me as if to say, 'Pet me! Let's play!' Having no kids of my own, or dogs, this was very unusual. As I sat in the park, I watched the river. I saw the sunlight glinting on the water. I heard and felt the wind rustling through the leaves of the trees, and I suddenly felt 'I get it.' The world is moving at a certain frequency, and I'm back in line with that frequency. From that moment on, things started to change in the outer world for me. They changed because I was clearing out old pain.

I am struck by Melanie's observation that she experienced the world around her in a fresh way. She was able to sense that the children, the dogs, the nature around her all had energy, and that she was receiving that energy. This occurred just as Melanie was starting to clean out her emotional cobwebs, which, in turn, allowed energy to flow more freely through her and into her. Much around the same time, I had similar experiences in my work with Arnie Kolodner—my own energy healer. Arnie was then a stage performer in New York who frequently played the romantic lead in the wildly popular Off-Broadway comedies of Charles Busch. Few people knew that he moonlighted as an Energy Healer. I saw Arnie maybe eight or nine times over a three-year period in the mid-nineties. These sessions changed how I know energy, and how I experience myself in my body.

Allow me to give you a little taste. I would hop on the N train at Astor Place in the East Village and head uptown, to Arnie's loft-like apartment in Clinton (we still called it Hell's Kitchen back then). I would lie on a massage table in Arnie's living-room, under a sky-light that afforded a rare Manhattan view of the sun and the clouds. Arnie would move his hands around the perimeters of my body. He moved and sensed energy but never actually touched any part of my body. When Arnie found places in my body that were blocked, he lingered and began to clear out energy that needed to be removed. And he urged me to talk. What came out of my mouth were usually extreme rants of anger and rage. Really old stuff, much of it coming from my very early childhood. I have no recollection of the words I uttered. All I know is that when I left Arnie and hopped back onto the N train, I was physically and emotionally drained. I have never experienced an exorcism, but I consider the sessions with Arnie my exorcisms. When I entered my apartment on Seventh Street I would pull the door shut and crawl straight into bed. I usually couldn't move for the rest of the day. I was completely wiped out!

The morning after, I invariably felt lighter. I want to say inexplicably lighter, but it's really quite explicable. Just like Mela-nie, I was beginning to release energy blocks within me and creat-ing space that allowed new energy to move in. I was starting to feel a tad different inside of my body—I was beginning to get a taste of the lightness of being!

When I think of these experiences I flash back to Wilhelm Reich, a radical figure in the world of psychiatry. Reich explicitly based his entire framework for understanding human behavior on the notion of blocked energy. He believed that folks who experi-enced significant challenges in life did so because their energy was stuck. Reich asserted the presence of a cosmic energy much like the *prana* or life force. He called it *orgone*. Reich maintained that every patient he saw came to him with physical blocks that had been established in childhood. A cure meant the removal of these physical blocks so the *orgone* could flow freely.

KUNDALINI ENERGY

The year of my first Arnie session is also the year I first heard about kundalini. That's a Sanskrit term for the really "big energy." Mythology says that this energy sits coiled at the base of our spine, waiting to be awakened. It rests there, dormant. We all have it. When it is awakened, it rises from its place at the base of the spine up through a narrow channel within the spine and out through the top of the head. As it does so, it awakens the energy centers that line our spine. Most commonly known as the chakras, these centers are the energy plugs for our sexual, emotional, and spiritual well-being. When these centers are open and clear, energy flows freely and fills us with a radiant sense of well-being.

If you haven't experienced kundalini, you might think that the folks who have are a bunch of whacked-out lunatics. I invite you to suspend disbelief. I have learned that I don't know what I don't know until I know it. Carl Jung, for example—one of the giants of modern psychological thought—was quite familiar with kundalini. In a marvelous filmed interview, Jung speaks in detail about a twenty-seven-year-old woman who came to him for help. "I have a snake in my abdomen," were the first words this patient uttered. Jung realized at once that she was referring to the image of the coiled serpent, the primal symbol of dormant kundalini energy. By the fifth session, the woman described that the snake had risen to the middle of her chest. By the tenth and final session, she stated that the snake had left through her mouth and that her head was filled with golden light. Jung's patient experienced her kundalini awakening right under his watch! Jung explained her experience through his analytical lens—the woman was highly intuitive and

LEVEL FOUR: ENERGY CONQUERS ALL

connecting with the collective unconscious. But Jung understood that the collective unconscious, in this case, was expressing itself in a symbol from Indian mythology![12]

Here's the most frustrating part about kundalini for an action-driven individual (and I definitely belong to this tribe): We cannot make the kundalini experience happen. We cannot will it into existence. There are only three ways of uncorking this "big energy:" We can facilitate kundalini release through a diligent practice of meditation, visualization, conscious breathing and chanting, ideally under the tutelage of a seasoned teacher. We can find a community or teacher who performs shaktipat, a ritual that temporarily awakens the kundalini energy for us and gives us a taste of the kundalini experience. Or, much like Jung's patient, we may be blessed by a spontaneous kundalini awakening, which is most likely to occur during times of high personal duress or in states of extreme relaxation. In both of these states, our guard is down and allows the kundalini to rise.

This is the first energy lesson, and it's the big lesson about the fourth level of connection: We cannot force it. We can activate it through intentional thought—but above all, we need to allow it and get out of the way.

I will describe my own kundalini experience in a little bit of detail. I do so because it matches how many others experience this energy. I do so also to whet your appetite for experiencing energy in unfamiliar ways. But above all, I do it because I firmly believe that once we have a richer experience of energy, we begin to have richer connections with others.

I received shaktipat and had a spontaneous kundalini awakening in the very same year. The spontaneous awakening occurred on a hillside above Thalheim, an obscure rural area of Germany an hour-and-a-half north of Frankfurt. I was alone. What is remarkable about Thalheim and its surroundings is just how utterly unremarkable it is. Thalheim doesn't show up in any guidebook for Germany travelers. It's beautiful in the most

ordinary kind of way. A cluster of small villages surrounds slop-
ing hills and corn fields. A country chapel hovers on a moun-
taintop. Wanderwege (the ubiquitous German hiking paths)
slice through these fields and cut through forests. The equally
ubiquitous wooden lookout towers hover above the corn fields
and provide sweeping views.

When I sat down on a bench overlooking the village of Thalheim,
the energy started to beam into me. It rose up from the scrotum, subtle first, but then insistent, as if I was plugged into an electric energy
socket. That sounds like such an obvious metaphor as I jot it down,
but that was truly what it felt like. I was plugged into some kind of
source, and the energy was streaming in and up my spine, and as it
rose, it spread wide into my entire torso. At the same time it felt as
if the top of my head and forehead had burst wide open, and light
was pouring in from above me. It was brilliant white light, and it just
kept flooding down into my body. It was as if I was sitting under a
warm shower of light. The light reminded me of images of Jesus that
I had seen which show him in a white pool of light descending from
heaven.

None of this experience required any sort of thought or effort
on my part. It was entirely visceral. This energy was bold. It was
undeniable. I was fully "in" my body and, at the same time, fully
connected to the entire world around me. Soon it felt like waves of
energy were washing over me and through me. These waves ebbed
and flowed, just like the waves that roll over me when I lie in the
Atlantic Ocean at Hollywood Beach during low tide. The waves
created gentle but persistent tremors throughout my body. I am
putting words to an experience that was entirely wordless, but I
trust the gist of what I experienced is clear.

I don't intend to glorify mystical experiences in this book. I have
had a few. They inspire awe. They can become quite addictive—
it's easy to become an energy-bliss-seeker. Big energy experiences
matter primarily because they offer us a glimpse of a different way
of knowing the world. They are one of the ways in which we pry

open our energy channels. They create a new muscle memory for what is possible in the world!

OUR ENERGY FRONTIER

Here's what we will explore for the remainder of this chapter: On the spectrum between the small and simple energy moment (I notice light as it falls onto a river) and the very big one (I feel waves of energy that wash like tidal waves through my body), there are many, many ways of accessing and experiencing energy. The marvelous thing is—there are just as many specific techniques to help us do so. They're readily available. All that's required is a desire to learn them. If you are drawn to the Chinese experience of chi, for example, there are practices that foster this experience of chi. Tai chi, qi gong, reiki, acupuncture. We will take a look at some of the ways in which we can access our energy reservoirs. We will see how this eventually leads to the ultimate reward in our relationships with others: the experience of flow.

I promised to keep this simple. Here's a simple story. In a public speaking class that I teach every summer for graduate students at the University of Massachusetts, we talk about energy. I often ask this question:

"How do we know that someone has energy?"

In my most recent class, Matilda, a sweet-faced young woman with an incandescent smile, raises her hand at once. "They're alive," she says.

That's it, isn't it?

So, for the remainder of this chapter, this is what we'll do: We will take a peek at what we can do to turn on our light and be radiantly alive!

UNLOCKING THE CHAKRAS

All roads lead back to the chakras.

Writing *Infectious* taught me this lesson, once and for all. When I began to write this book, a question popped up in my brain, almost at once: Do I really need to talk about the chakras again? Aren't they "old news" by now? I first learned about the chakras in the late 1980s, when I attended the Louise Hay Healing Circles in downtown Manhattan. The work of Louise Hay centers on the simple belief that any physical discomfort, large or small, is a symbol of a deeper psychic imbalance. A major tenet of the Louise Hay approach to wellness is that we listen to our bodies and pay attention. And the chakras are one of the premier doorways to our physical well-being, our energy, our spirit.

As I look back, I realize how much I have taken my relationship to the chakras for granted. I often do a spontaneous chakra clearing when I feel tension or stress. I frequently experience energy streaming into my body through one chakra or multiple chakras. At times, this is an unexpected visitation. At other times it is something I invoke. I experience energy in my chakras with a special intensity when I chant and meditate.

No matter how my energy manifests—I have an active relationship with my chakras. Much of it happens without a great deal of thought on my part any more. At its best, it's a marvelous example of muscle memory. But with the chakras, it's easy to suddenly become one of those jaded New York City subway riders who's taken the A train once too often. You know—the one who sits down and doesn't pay attention to his surroundings anymore. That's when he suddenly misses a stop or two and ends up in an entirely different part of town!

So—let's pay attention. If you're new to the chakras, welcome to a simple and immensely rewarding map for accessing your personal energy. If you're already familiar with the chakras, consider what you may stand to discover by revisiting the chakra fundamentals.

We will take a brief look at the functions of each of our seven chakras. We will explore ways in which we can begin to access the energy that flows through each of the chakras. And we will identify how our connection with the chakras will help us to better connect with folks in absolutely any situation.

THE FUNCTIONS OF THE SEVEN CHAKRAS

Table 7: The locations of the chakras

The seven major chakras are energy centers that line our spine, beginning at its base and leading up to the crown of our head (Table 7). Imagine that each chakra is a funnel of energy whose vortex rests inside of your body, along the spinal cord. The spinal cord acts as an energy highway that allows energy to move from the base to the top of the head and out. It also facilitates the movement of energy from the crown of the head down into the body. Each chakra attracts a different color of light or energy, and each is associated with a different aspect of our well-being. The bottom and top chakras are considered the two polar balancing chakras—the bottom one connects us to the energy of the earth, the source of all living things. It roots and ground us. The top chakra connects us with the world of spirit and the divine.

Let's take a closer look at each chakra and just how it channels energy for us.

FIRST CHAKRA – THE ROOT CHAKRA

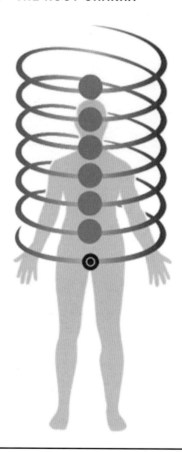

Location: Base of the Spine
Color: Red
Function: The first chakra provides energy for our physical health, vitality, and a sense of being grounded. It is our connection to the earth and the earth energy—the source of everything that grows and blossoms. It is often called the energy of survival and stability. It is a source of courage and self-confidence.
When it is blocked: We tend to hold onto anger and rage in the first chakra.

SECOND CHAKRA – THE SEX CHAKRA

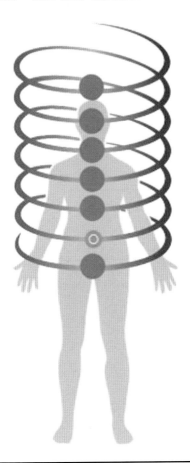

Location: Pubic Area/Sexual Organs
Color: Orange
Function: The second chakra fuels our sexual energy and our creativity. It connects us to the five senses and removes our inhibitions. It is the energy of full self-expression. The color orange is also associated with friendly and warm behavior.
When it is blocked: We may become manipulative or turn into excessive power-seekers.

THIRD CHAKRA – THE POWER CHAKRA

Location: Navel Center/Solar Plexus
Color: Yellow
Function: The third chakra influences our sense of self and self-esteem. It fuels our personality, ego, and our concern with how others perceive us. It champions our intellect, clear thinking, and the ability to make sense of things. Wisdom and clarity are strong attributes of an open third chakra.
When it is blocked: We may have a lot of personal inhibitions or display a pedantic, overly-intellectual approach to life.

FOURTH CHAKRA – THE HEART CHAKRA

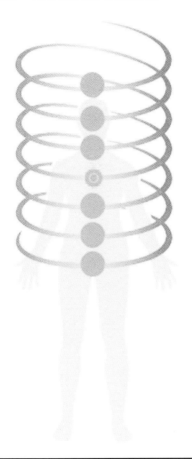

<u>Location:</u> Heart	
<u>Color:</u> Green	
<u>Function:</u> The fourth chakra unlocks our ability to feel love, compassion, and empathy. When this chakra is balanced, we are able to give love and at the same time love and nurture ourselves. With an open fourth chakra we experience a deep sense of peace and harmony.	
<u>When it is blocked:</u> We are prone to experiencing a lot of fear and quick mood swings. We resort to domineering and overly critical behavior.	

FIFTH CHAKRA – THE COMMUNICATION CHAKRA

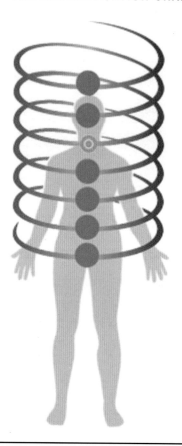

<u>Location</u>: Pit of the Throat	

<u>Color</u>: Blue	

<u>Function</u>: The fifth chakra supports our ability to communicate clearly, express ourselves well, and speak the truth. It allows us to effectively influence situations. This chakra makes it possible for us to tell others what we need. When it is open, we choose our words well and make it easy for others to hear us.

<u>When it is blocked</u>: We stop expressing our thoughts and feelings and "shut down." We start to act brusque or arrogant and show disdain for the perspectives of others.

SIXTH CHAKRA – THE WISDOM CHAKRA

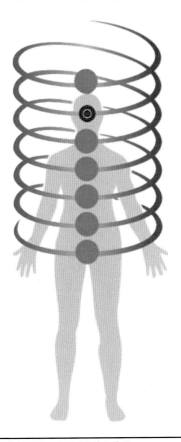

Location: Center of the Forehead/Third Eye	
Color: Indigo	
Function: The sixth chakra connects us to our intuition and gut instincts, and it activates our psychic powers. It is the link to our unconscious self and, at the same time, helps us to feel connected to the entire world around us. When the sixth chakra is open, we see situations from a more enlightened perspective. It also helps us to remember our dreams.	
When it is blocked: We may feel depressed, confused, or mentally "clouded."	

SEVENTH CHAKRA – THE DIVINE CHAKRA

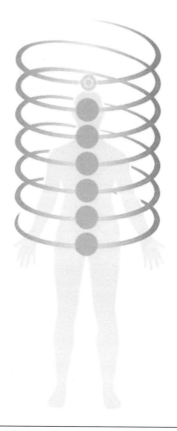

<u>Location</u>: Crown of the Head
<u>Color</u>: Violet
<u>Function</u>: The seventh chakra is our connection to spiritual abundance and the divine. When it is open, we feel a profound union with our higher self and our higher consciousness. The violet energy invokes wisdom and inner strength. It gives us inspiration in all of our undertakings. Like the second chakra, it also fosters creative unfolding.
<u>When it is blocked</u>: As in the sixth chakra, imbalances may show up as depression. We feel frustrated with not expressing our true nature and potential.

This is a simple overview of the seven major energy vortices in our body. As you focus your attention on the upper chakras along the spine, you may discover that you are sensing or attracting white light instead of the violet or blue lights. Wonderful. The four lower chakras are associated with the four earthly elements—earth, water, fire, and air. The three upper chakras are not associated with any earthly elements; they draw energy from the spiritual world. White light is the brilliant energy of electromagnetic fields, commonly called auras. It transcends the energy of our seven chakras. This light is the source of a deep inner radiance that other people may sense in you, even when they do not see your aura. So—if you are attracting white light in and around you, enjoy it! You are connecting with a transcendent energy that will touch you and, in turn, those who are in your presence.

HOW WE CAN ACCESS ENERGY THROUGH THE CHAKRAS

1. **Desire the experience.**

   The Chakra System is an ancient framework for understanding and accessing personal energy and has been around for thousands of years. If you have doubts about the chakras because they seem a little foreign—cool. If you dismiss them entirely, you are also dismissing any opportunity of experiencing the powerful energy that travels through the chakras.

   Here's how you begin: Desire to know the chakra experience! Be curious about it. When you approach the chakras with this intent, you will accelerate your own ability to access and experience energy.

2. **Work with a teacher.**

   To start, avail yourself of a master teacher who can help you to experience and release energy. Acupuncturists, reflexologists, qi gong masters, energy healers, reiki practitioners are all folks who have been trained to help you access energy—

directly or indirectly—through your body. Their skills will provide your body with an increasingly tangible and repeatable experience of energy. You will gain a clearer sense of what energy flow in your body feels like.

3. **Pay attention to your body.**

Our culture rewards us for being smart. If your success in this world has been built around your smarts—terrific. There's a good chance, however, that your brain may often be cut off from what the rest of your body is experiencing. This may mean a separation from emotions—especially the not so pleasant ones—and a separation from anything other than your mental energy. Separation may mean that I am simply not aware of something that is going on in my body. It may also mean that I prevent it from occurring in the first place. I block that which I do not like. I shut down.

"The body is the shortcut to everything that goes on inside of us," says Melanie Hahn Roche. "Notice what you are feeling. Name it and say it. Track it. It will help you to have more empathy with yourself, and it will also help you to have empathy with others."

It is nearly impossible to know energy if we don't pay attention to the sensations within our body. So—start tracking what your body tells you. Your attention will be rewarded!

4. **Learn the chakra basics.**

Find the locations of the seven primary chakras in your body. You may wish to place a finger or hand on them. Make their locations specific and real for yourself.

Learn the colors of each chakra. You may wish to use the overview I have provided in this chapter. Learn, also, the primary purpose of each chakra. This is the "language of the chakras," and it is helpful to know it as you begin to deliberately access your energy centers.

5. Conduct your own chakra tune-up.

Once you have a sense of where your chakras are located, begin to perform a chakra tune-up. Just like a car engine benefits from regular maintenance, so does your energy system!

Sit or lie down in a comfortable and private space. You do not need to sit in a yoga position, with your legs crossed. It is crucial, however, that your spine is straight and elongated—this, after all, is the highway that your energy travels.

Take several deep breaths, down into your abdomen. Use the abdomen as a pump that draws breath into your body and pushes it back out. As your breath deepens, feel it traveling up and down your spine, as well. You are beginning to activate your energy centers!

Focus your attention on one chakra at a time. Begin with the root chakra. Visualize its color (red). Visualize the color all around the location of the chakra. Visualize, as well, energy streaming into your body through the chakra. See the energy in the color of the chakra. Continue to breathe, keep your eyes closed, and visualize the energy entering your body at the chakra location.

Repeat the same process for the second chakra—your sex chakra. There is no guideline for how much time you spend with a chakra. If you feel like you are not connecting with a specific chakra—relax. Turn your attention back to your breathing. Inhale and exhale deeply. Send breath to the chakra you're focusing on.

When you are done, proceed to the remaining five chakras, moving your way up the spine, one chakra at a time. Repeat the same process with each chakra. End with the crown chakra—your divine chakra.

You may find that you experience some chakras quite strongly, others not at all. No worries. Consider it helpful information about an aspect of yourself that would benefit from a bit more energy.

6. Experiment with symbolic imagery.

Part of the pleasure of exploring the chakras is finding the imagery that "does the trick" for you. I use the image of a tornado, much like the tornadoes we see during natural disasters or in disaster movies like "Twister." I visualize a tornado-like whirlwind hovering over a chakra, in the color that is associated with that chakra. I then feel that tornado making contact with by body and beaming into me. I see the tornado whirling, twirling, and drilling into me.

I like the image of a tornado because of the natural power associated with it. It offers more than a mere polite infusion of energy—it showers me with a roaring blast!

I have also learned that the bottom and top chakras, because of their location, have only one point of entry. The other five chakras that line my spine can be entered from both the front and the back of my body. We tend to visualize the energy moving into the spine from the front portion of the body. When I summon the tornado energy, I summon it on both sides of my spine. It is an even more potent way of drawing energy into my body and balancing it, at the same time.

Please pay attention to any other symbols that may represent energy for you. Early in my chakra explorations I noticed that when I focused on my sixth chakra—the Wisdom Chakra—an image of an inverted pyramid would appear. I discovered, as well, that this image quickly connected me with images, memories, insights that my conscious mind could not access. So in the evening, as I lay down in bed and prepared to go to sleep, I began to visualize my inverted pyramid right over my third eye. What delicious visions and dreams that invoked!

HOW THE CHAKRAS CAN HELP IN EVERYDAY SITUATIONS

This is the beauty of "speaking the chakra language:" Once the chakras have become a familiar way of understanding our body and how we access energy, they are available to assist us in pretty much any situation. Here are some examples:

You are having a chat with a colleague who is upset with you.	
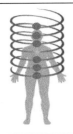	**Your chakra helper:** Focus on your fourth chakra—your heart chakra. **Action:** Draw special energy and light into your heart center. This energy will help you to not get triggered, and it will help your colleague to simmer down.

You are giving an important business pitch to key business stakeholders.	
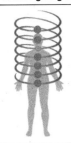	**Your chakra helper:** Focus on your fifth chakra—your communication chakra. **Action:** When you draw energy into your fifth chakra, you unlock your channels of communication. Consider drawing extra energy into your third chakra, as well. This strengthens your sense of personal power and confidence. That's a potent energy combination!

You are struggling with making a difficult decision.	
	**Your chakra helper:** Focus on your sixth chakra—the wisdom chakra. **Action:** As you draw energy to the center of your forehead, breathe and notice what insights may be revealed. Be open to the language of these insights—they may come in the guise of an image, a hunch, a recurring word. Just notice!

149

You feel overwhelmed with too many things coming at you.	
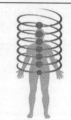	<u>Your chakra helper:</u> Focus on your first chakra—the root chakra.
	<u>Action:</u> Several chakras could be helpful here, but whenever you feel a little "off-center," draw energy to the chakra that will center you. Yes, that's the root chakra. Find yourself instantly calming down as you draw red energy to the base of your spine.

Consider this another invaluable gift of learning to tune our chakras: We can conduct our tune-up before we have a conversation that is important to us—it will alter the energy we bring to the conversation. We can also fine-tune our chakras in the middle of a conversation. When you find yourself getting upset, distracted, rattled, scattered—send energy to the chakra that will give you the specific energy you most need. What you do will be invisible to those around you—but it will alter your energy while you're in the midst of a chat. And even though your conversation partners may not be able to name it, they will "know it." That's pretty powerful!

THREE MORE ENERGY PATHWAYS

I think of the chakras as the super-highway to charging yourself with energy. There are other scenic routes that will get you there, as well. Consider this section your map to a few of the other routes. I'm a map guy, and I have loved maps ever since I was a little boy; they have led me to a magical spot or two. If any of the roads on this map entice you, consider getting into the car and going for a ride. Whichever path you choose—it will be a richly satisfying trip.

A quick reflection before we hit the road. In Western pop culture, we tend to avoid a deeper conversation about the energy experience. We like to define human behavior by cognitive personality models. Carl Jung's division of personality types into introverts and extroverts still serves as the most prevalent notion of how we access energy. Introverts, according to Jung, tend to derive energy from thoughts and ideas while extroverts tend to derive it from other people. To this day, Jung's introversion/extroversion duality remains the benchmark for defining differences in how individuals access and experience energy. Since Jung's passing in 1961, his work has further infiltrated our collective consciousness via personality profiles such as the ubiquitous *MBTI* (Myers-Briggs-Type-Indicator).

I am glad no one subjected me to a personality profile when I was in high school. On the introversion/extroversion scale, I likely would have registered off-the-charts on the introversion side. To this day, I have a strong private side that enjoys occasional solitude, writing, walks in nature, reading a book. I have an equally strong public side that relishes lively chats with stimulating people, group sports, team brainstorms. My entire professional life is played out in public interactions and affords me great pleasure. I no longer terribly much care which side—to use psychological parlance—is my adapted style, which my original one. It's an irrelevant question. I draw energy from people. Lots and lots of it. And I draw energy from my thoughts. Lots and lots of it.

Let me be very clear. We're post-Jung in this book. The chakras are for everyone. The roads on this map are for everyone. The techniques in these pages have enriched introverts and extroverts. If your personal narrative tells you that you're not one of those people that can access this kind of energy—toss that narrative! If your psychological assessment tells you that you tend to think and not feel or intuit—well, do with that information what you want, but just for now, disregard it. Please! The energy we speak of is bigger than these labels. It is bigger than introversion and extroversion. It's available to all of us. Your ability to access it will change how you connect with absolutely anybody in your life.

We'll start with neuro-linguistic programming, a mundane path. We will end with Power Animals, a mystical one. And there's a whole wide ocean of *chi* in between.

NEURO-LINGUISTIC PROGRAMMING (NLP)

I wish it had been called something different. Neuro-linguistic programming (we'll refer to it as NLP, for short) is an annoyingly academic name for a rather intuitive approach to establishing rapport with another person. NLP first burst into prominence in the late 1970s and seems to have peaked in popularity in the 1990s. It is based on a body of research that has been vilified by critics almost from the moment it burst onto the scene. Critics not withstanding—NLP techniques are simple and work!

NLP offers specific tools for "getting in sync" with the energy of another person. Here's a word of caution. NLP techniques are very concrete. That is both a gift and a curse. My colleague Jayne Warrilow, a marvelous executive coach who assists her clients in establishing resonant connections, describes this conundrum as follows: "NLP takes a very technical, bite-sized approach to how we connect with people. By putting such specific language around something as vast as human rapport and energy, we immediately confine what it is."

I concur. I think of NLP as "energy lite." Nevertheless—here are four "lite" techniques that you may find helpful:

1. **Use strategic verbal cues.**

   Our choice of language triggers the emotions and thought patterns of another person. We know from our chapter on "Telling Stories" that when we use sensory cue words, our listener will connect to hidden memories and emotions that are triggered by our sensory language.

   Our conversation partner, in turn, tends to tell us if he processes information through visual, auditory, or kinesthetic means. His verbal cues let us know if he makes sense of things in a primarily visual ("yes, I can see that"), auditory ("yes, that sounds great"), or kinesthetic manner ("yes, that feels wonderful"). When we choose verbal cues that match how he processes information, we fast-forward our connection with him.

2. Match their breath.

Notice how a person is breathing. We are able to accelerate our connection with folks when we notice the rhythm of their breath. Do they breathe rapidly? Do they breathe leisurely? When we adjust the rhythm of our breathing to match theirs, we are suddenly "on the same wavelength." We strengthen the unspoken connection with the person.

3. Mirror their nonverbal signals.

Do not stop at matching their verbal cues and breathing. Notice the body language of your conversation partner. Notice her speech rhythm, the degree of facial animation, the amount of gestures. By subtly mirroring some of these signals, we find ourselves more in synch with the other person. Subtlety is the keyword when it comes to mirroring!

4. Anchor yourself.

Anchoring techniques are quick physical and mental adjustments we make to center ourselves. These techniques help us to be in touch with our own energy; this, in turn, allows us to more fully receive the energy of others.

Focused breathing, positive affirmations, visualization, prayer, and the ability to invoke a sensory cue that we associate with a pleasant moment in our life all have the power to put us in a great state of mind. They are but a few of the ways in which we can anchor ourselves.

I salute NLP for its explicit take on the introversion/extroversion duality. According to NLP, no one is genetically pre-wired to be an introvert or an extrovert. Introversion and extroversion—and the associated habits with which we experience energy—are meta-programs (to use NLP terminology) that we acquired from our parents, teachers, and the culture in which we grew up. They are tendencies that we have solidified in childhood, not core personality traits. More importantly, our experiences in adult life can significantly change these tendencies. A resounding YES to this perspective!

ACTIVATING YOUR *CHI*

"Can anybody access *chi*?" I ask Dr. Isaac Goren. His answer is unequivocal: "Yes." I press on, just to be sure: "So absolutely everyone—shy, introverted people, non-high-energy people—can access *chi*?" "Yes."

Chi is the Chinese term for our life force. Its presence is the underlying principle for all Chinese medicine. Unlike the kundalini energy (a Sanskrit term) which we access through our chakras along the spine, *chi* travels through energy channels called meridians that crisscross our entire body. When these channels are open, they send *chi* to the vital organs within the body. I offer you a short glossary of different practices that facilitate the flow of *chi*. Consider them our *chi*-catalysts. Most of these are initially best practiced under the tutelage of a seasoned teacher. "Energy is like a muscle," says Jayne Warrilow. "It requires practice. We need to find space in our lives to be in an energy practice."

Here are seven concrete ways in which you can discover *chi* and start your energy practice:

1. **Acupuncture**

   During an acupuncture treatment, thin needles are inserted into acupuncture points in the skin. These points activate the flow of *chi* or correct imbalances in the flow of *chi*. When acupuncture is performed by a practitioner who correctly intuits where your *chi* needs to be strengthened, it will provide you with a palpable experience of what *chi* feels like.

2. Qi Gong

Qi gong is a physical and mental practice that strengthens or balances the *chi* in your body. It encompasses a range of styles that may have a primarily martial, medical, or spiritual focus. Regardless of the intent of your practice, all qi gong styles tend to include a strong attention to mental clarity, breathing techniques, and the repetition of postures. Besides helping you to better know your *chi*, qi gong is also likely to unlock your upper chakras and initiate higher levels of awareness.

3. Tai Chi

Tai chi is the abbreviated name for a slow-moving ancient Chinese martial arts form. Performed both solo and in partnership with another person, it requires the repetitive performance of a series of core movements in a graceful manner. It is considered a form of qi gong. During tai chi, the body is in constant motion as one posture flows into the next. Tai chi helps us to sense the *chi* within our body and the *chi* of the air around us.

4. Reiki

Reiki is the Japanese art of transferring energy from one person to another. A reiki practitioner uses the cupped palm of her hands to transfer *ki*, the Japanese word for *chi*, to the person she's tending to. *Ki* is often felt by the receiver in the form of heat and strong energy vibrations. It fosters a deep sense of peace and wellness.

5. Reflexology

A reflexologist applies pressure to a wide range of reflex points on the feet and hands. Just like needles in acupuncture, this pressure activates *chi* that is sent via meridians to specific organs inside your body. This release of *chi* helps to remove any energy blocks within the body and strengthens the function of the organs it is targeting. Reflexology offers us a tangible experience of *chi*—and it just plain feels good!

6. Alexander Technique

Alexander Technique is not intended as a chi-releasing technique. It teaches us to unlearn bad posture habits and returns us to a more natural, tension-free way of carrying our bodies. A big part of this realignment requires us to learn a new way of holding our spine, neck, and head. By realigning our spine, we're opening up our energy highway. Let the *chi* flow!

7. Yoga

A yoga class can be found in most decent fitness centers these days. Yoga is the ritualized practice of deep breathing and physical postures that stretch our body. While there are many different varieties of yoga, all yoga connects us to our *chi* through its focus on breath. As a side-benefit of our yoga practice, we often experience the world around us more brilliantly. We begin to "see" the energy that exists in the physical world.

Some of the just-mentioned techniques are primarily known as "alternative medicine" approaches to wellness and healing. Fine. But you don't need to have a physical ailment to try acupuncture. You don't need to have a liver dysfunction to try reflexology. You don't need to have a strain in your abdomen to try qi gong. Go to an acupuncturist just to experience your *chi* in balance. Take a yoga class just to plunge deeper into your breath. I can describe these experiences all I want; in the end, we need to experience the benefits of these practices in our body. I hope I am enticing you to run out and do just that. Try one of our seven *chi*-catalysts! You will instantly know your body in a fresh way. And when you know your body in a fresh way, you will connect with others in a fresh way. Guaranteed.

Power Animals

Many moons ago in acting class, we did animal exercises. Chances are, if you're an actor and went to an acting school, you had to do an animal exercise, as well. I felt a little silly and self-conscious at first, crawling around the floor of an acting studio and turning myself into a wild beast. I look back now and think "how wonderful!" In the guise of an animal, I had permission to make raw, guttural growls. I had permission to gesture broadly and move boldly. I had the chance to feel a ferocious, fearless power that I had never felt before, and I had permission to express this power with my entire body. Uncensored, untamed.

I connected with the primal energy I had been socialized to hide.

This is the same power that charismatic people channel with such ease. All Native American cultures incorporate this primal energy of animals into their world view. They call it "power animals." Power animals are viewed as spirits and energies that guide, protect, empower. Just as a chakra channels a very specific energy, each power animal offers a very particular kind of strength. Most importantly, power animals are believed to reside right inside of us. They are considered a vital source of our psychic energy. The Chinese Lunar Calendar names each year after one of twelve animals. The Chinese believe that the animal that rules the year in which we were born has a profound impact on your life. The saying goes that "this is the animal that lives in your heart."

Sound abstract? I didn't know about power animals until they showed up in my life, unannounced. Let me make this very concrete. Toward the end of 1989, I spent six weeks in the small Arizona town of Rimrock, about half an hour south of Sedona (this is the same place where Reverend Mona told me I was a doormat . . .). I lived on an abandoned dude ranch that sat atop an Anasazi burial mound. That should have been my first clue that animal spirits were around!

After a week of fasting, juicing, and detoxing, they came. I was on a break between my juice times and wandered down to a brook that ran along the base of the mound, just this side of a prairie

157

where a settlement of new houses sprawled. The water was clear and cool, and I planted my feet firmly in the riverbed. I stood right at the bend where the brook formed a little tub in the earth. My feet curled into the soft river mud and my eyes looked west to the corroding fence of a horse ranch when suddenly they appeared, a peacock, a bear, an eagle and a deer. They flashed for a moment, sharp and very clear, across the morning sky, then they vanished. The eagle rested on my head, the peacock walked towards me through the water, the deer and the bear stood on opposite sides of the riverbed and watched. This moment shivered across the brook, but I, of course, felt it shiver right down my spine. I had not yet studied the Native American Medicine Wheel or the symbolic meaning of Power Animals or the role of Shapeshifters. But this moment was unmistakable. It happened.

I know now that this was my first visitation by power animals.

I ran back to the river every day now. There's one place I loved above all the others. It's where the leopard came to visit me. I raced down the hill and crossed a mud-caked plateau, flung aside hip-high shrubs that broke at a touch. Then I stepped over a much stepped-over chicken-wire fence and descended into a narrow gorge. There was no water there anymore, and the earth in this gorge was dry. When I lay down I was no longer visible from the plain. I pressed my back into the pebbled ground, wiggled it until the fit was snug. The wind swooped through this hollow riverbed and rustled the earth. When I looked up I saw the split trunk of a tree, and branches that looped into spirals, and beyond it the vaulting sky.

The second I closed my eyes, he came. He always came alone. I lay with my eyes shut and felt the leopard rise from my crotch. He climbed on top of my chest, sat and sprawled and then covered the entire length of my body. He was not an image in my mind—no, this leopard had form and weight, a lot of weight, his energy shot straight into my limbs, pressed into me fast, it was a hot, surging kind of energy. My limbs quivered and fell with the force of his weight. I felt my flesh and my bones drop away, as if the leopard's belly were crushing me into the earth. I heard a lapping, hushing sound, I felt his hot breath sweep over my face. It was a breath of fire and rot and sweet, dangerous life. Leaves rustled and drubbed my face, and the weight seemed to shove me deeper and deeper into the earth, I felt the hot desert wind sweep over me, and then, suddenly, I was swallowed into the ground.

When I opened my eyes I saw the sky again. It suddenly seemed even more distant and vast and so brilliantly clear. And my body brimmed with a keen, racing energy that seemed impossible to contain.

Why does this matter, you may wonder?

If you are someone who is stirred by mythic imagery and symbols, power animals may be your link to vast reservoirs of energy. Study them. Find out about them. See if they speak to you. For me, power animals were my initiation into a reality I had not previously known. People who cherish this visionary world believe that it is the real world, and that everything else is a mere illusion. I won't quibble about it here. But of this I am certain: After feeling the presence of power animals, outside of me and within me, my world has never been the same. I see things around me differently. People, nature, buildings, the sky. I see myself differently. I am humbled.

In Rimrock, my eyes, my mind, and my heart were opened to energies which I didn't know existed. I dipped into the big jar of honey.

SUMMARY

"Energy" is the fourth and final level of connection. It is the realm where all connections that truly resonate unfold. I believe that as we know energy more consciously, we flow more consciously with the energy of another person.

Cultures throughout history have found language to describe energy. The most common phrase attributed to it is "life force." The Hindus call it *prana*, the Japanese *ki*, the Chinese *qi* or *chi*.

There are almost 100 other names associated with this energy in as many different cultures. Breath, and the way we breathe, is by most cultures viewed as the source of this original life force.

Our experience of energy can range from a simple moment in nature (we notice light as it falls onto a river) to a large, transcendent experience (we feel waves of energy that wash like tidal waves through our body). There are many, many ways of accessing and experiencing energy. There are just as many specific techniques to help us do so. They're readily available. All that's required is a desire to learn them.

Unlocking the Chakras

The seven chakras are energy centers that line our spine, beginning at its base and leading up to the crown of our head. Each chakra is a funnel of energy whose vortex rests inside of your body, along the spinal cord. The spinal cord acts as an energy highway that allows energy to move from the base to the top of the head and out. There are specific techniques for unlocking the chakras that anyone can learn.

Applying NLP

Neuro-linguistic Programming (NLP) is a concrete approach to noticing the verbal and energetic cues of another person. By mirroring and matching the cues we receive, we get on the same wavelength with the other person and accelerate the connection. We end up being in synch. This is especially effective when we use anchoring techniques. When we anchor ourselves, we make sure that we're fully present in any given moment. We are in touch with our own energy!

Activating Our *Chi*

Chi is the Chinese term for life force. Its presence is the underlying principle for all Chinese medicine. *Chi* travels through energy channels called meridians that crisscross our entire body. When these channels are open, they send *chi* to the vital organs within the body. There are many different practices that facilitate the flow of *chi*—acupuncture, qi gong, tai chi, reflexology, reiki, Alexander Technique, yoga. Most of these are initially best practiced under the tutelage of a seasoned teacher.

Connecting with Power Animals

If you are stirred by symbols and mythic imagery, power animals may be your fast track to vast hidden energies. All Native American cultures incorporate the primal energy of animals into their world view. They call it "power animals." Power animals are spirits and energies that guide, protect, empower. They are believed to reside right inside of us. The Chinese Lunar Calendar names each year after one of twelve animals. The Chinese believe that the animal that rules the year in which we were born "is the animal that lives in your heart."

Epilogue
Getting to Mastery

I hope that as you reach this part of *Infectious*, you're reveling in the fact that a satisfying connection with another person plays on multiple levels. It plays on these levels all at the same time. These levels are both visible and invisible. The truly resonant connections tend to happen on the invisible planes. Yes, this can indeed feel daunting. Rejoice! The Four Levels of Connection are our simple roadmap for mastering the seemingly elusive threads of a human connection (Table 8). We know it well by now.

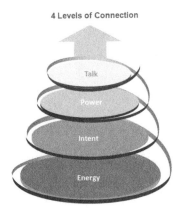

4 Levels of Connection

Talk

Power

Intent

Energy

Table 8: What I put out into the world

I have placed most of our attention in this book on the choices we make in a social situation. After all—we have no control over what the other person chooses to do. But here's what it looks like when two people engage:

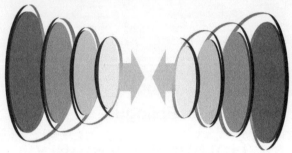

Table 9: When two people play

The layers start to look pretty complex now, don't they? Let's take this into a group situation, and the dynamics can suddenly seem truly dizzying:

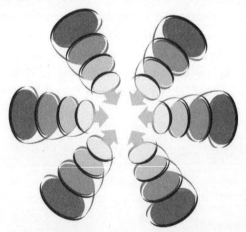

Table 10: When a group gets together

It would be preposterous to try and master every dynamic that goes on in such a gathering. We have invented the term "control freak" to describe the person that attempts to do just that. No, when we consider mastery, we're considering the ease and skill with which we play on our four levels. Our ease will, in turn, potently influence how everyone around us acts and reacts!

THE BEAUTY OF PRACTICE

When I think of the word "mastery," I think of sports, martial arts, meditation. I think of hobbies I'm passionate about. I also think of writing, and the actions I took when I first decided that I wished to write. I studied with some truly marvelous writing teachers in New York City. I wrote, wrote, and then I wrote some more.

Yes, I think of practice. Lots and lots of practice.

Mastery takes time—and as it is, most of us never seem to have enough time in any given day to do everything we wish to do. Just as the break-neck pace of our daily lives conspires against establishing a deeper connection with folks, it also conspires against mastery. Research, furthermore, consistently shows that with any skill that requires substantial practice, getting to mastery is not a neat, steady ascent. It's a long haul. A burst of growth and a sense of improvement are followed by long stretches of "plateau-ing" which are eventually followed by another burst of growth and improvement. Dedicated athletes know when a plateau is coming. They continue to practice during the plateau. They know that "riding out" the plateau eventually leads to another spurt of growth. Less committed folks are more likely to throw in the towel.

Practice in a sport or hobby is easy, in a way. We create dedicated time for it. We may resent the effort it requires, but we are just as likely quite pleased to have this special time where we stop doing anything else. We have a singular focus on a very specific task (though every time I go to my gym I am startled by how many folks are unable to commit to dedicated gym time without stopping every few minutes to send a text message or check their voice mails . . .). Especially when the task requires physical exertion, we feel the fruit of our efforts when we're finished. Even when the fruit is pain or soreness or exhaustion, the outcome is tangible. We "know it" in the body!

STAYING FRESH

The question of mastery takes on a whole new meaning with this Guinness World Record. On September 1, 2011, George Lee Andrews left the Broadway production of *The Phantom of the Opera* after appearing in it since it first opened on January 26, 1988. This twenty-three-year run in the same show makes Andrews the longest-running performer in a single show in Broadway history. During his tenure, Andrews switched in and out of four different roles. It is safe to assume that Andrews quickly mastered the mechanics of each role—the staging, the dialogue, the delivery of the songs at a high professional level. As a principal in a Broadway show, he was working under standard six-month contracts. If Andrews had not demonstrated a basic level of mastery, his contract would not have been renewed. It was renewed over forty times.

In a twenty-three-year run, mastery is assumed. This is the question everyone asked Mr. Andrews after his departure: "How the heck did you manage to keep your performances fresh?"

Mr. Andrews' answers are illuminating. He created rituals that he performed before each performance. He recited poetry to himself. He always touched a certain set piece with a cane. Rituals helped him to get centered in the present moment. He also set himself different challenges each week. Some weeks he focused on his breathing, at other times on the comedy of the performance. Think of them as Mr. Andrews' conscious little experiments.

While Mr. Andrews stayed constant in his roles, new performers continued to rotate in and out of the roles around him. Couple this with the fact that in most weeks, understudies filled in for one or several of the regular performers who were sick or on vacation, and the cast, night after night, was never entirely the same. This allowed Mr. Andrews to respond to new stage relationships, fresh energy. And the one big variable that changed every night—the audience. Their mood, their energy, their responses. The beauty of knowing your lines and songs inside out is that it's no longer about knowing your lines and songs inside out. It's about noticing what's fresh, unexpected, surprising beyond the lines and songs.

Mr. Andrews boiled it down to this: "It's a technique—to do what you're supposed to do but approach it in a fresh way. It's about staying concentrated in the moment of the character and moving through the play. That's Acting 101. So when I walk onstage, I don't ever feel un-fresh. I always let my characters burst into a new situation."[13]

MUSCLE MEMORY IN DAILY LIFE

This is the wonder of achieving mastery of our Four Levels: Unless you're a hermit, you have conversations all the time. Life requires that you, every day, engage in the very thing you seek to master. You have the brilliant opportunity to practice every day, all the time, any time you want!

In his book *Mastery: The Keys to Success and Long-Term Fulfillment*, venerated journalist and martial artist George Leonard writes about all the ways in which we neglect the opportunities for mastery in our everyday life:

> Our preoccupation with goals, results, and the quick fix has separated us from our own experiences. To put it more starkly, it has robbed us of countless hours of the time of our lives. We awaken in the morning and hurry to get dressed. (Getting dressed doesn't count.) We hurry to eat breakfast so that we can get to work. (Eating breakfast doesn't count.) We hurry

to get to work. (Getting to work doesn't count.) Maybe work will be interesting and satisfying and we won't simply have to endure it while waiting for lunchtime to come. And maybe lunch will bring a warm, intimate meeting, with fascinating conversation. But maybe not.[14]

Practice, in everyday life, is not the ambitious, goal-driven, effort-laden, sweating buckets, win-a-competition kind of practice. Mastery of the Four Levels is not a hard hustle. It is the "let me see how I can stay fresh approach" Mr. Andrews speaks of. It's a gentle practice. It is born of small, deliberate, effortless experiments. It is fueled by a steady mindfulness. It unfolds with grace. The prize is our enjoyment of a deeper connection with folks. The prize, quite simply, is a more satisfying life.

Muscle memory is the reward of our devotion to practice—in a physical activity, and in our Four Levels. The hands of a pianist who have practiced a Chopin étude for hundreds of hours will start fingering imaginary piano keys the moment the etude plays on the radio. That's muscle memory in action. The gift of such memory? When the pianist sits down at a piano to play Chopin, his attention no longer goes to the technical execution of the musical score. He, instead, expresses the artistic inspiration of a particular moment. That's when Chopin truly comes alive!

The beauty of muscle memory in the Four Levels? Our small, deliberate experiments bring us to the point where the skills of this book become "second nature" for us. We ask curiosity questions, we tell our stories, we reframe, we charge our power plugs, we speak with intent, we consistently choose to access our energy. We do all of this with ease and little deliberation. We trust our skills. Because we trust our skills, we trust our instincts. Because we trust our instincts, we are able to pay attention to what's going on around us. We intuitively know how to engage with pretty much anybody. The Four Levels have become a way of life.

That's when "flow" happens.

WHEN IT FLOWS

You know those moments when a conversation unfolds without effort? When words seem to tumble with an untamable excitement from our lips? When we can hardly wait to continue the thread of a conversation? When it feels so completely wonderful to be in that particular place, in that conversation, in that moment, with that person? When we feel like we have known our conversation mate forever even though it's the first time we're having a chat? When we suddenly lose all sense of time?

That's flow.

What is it that flows, you may ask? (Yes, it might be liquor, but let's entertain the liquor-free version right now, shall we . . .) We sometimes call it chemistry. We call it inspiration. Let's just keep it simple and call it energy.

I used to think that moments of flow were the magical little gifts that life sometimes grants us. Well, they are. But ever since I discovered the research that Mihalyi Csikszentmihalyi conducted on the nature of flow, I realize that some folks experience a lot more flow than others. In his classic book *Flow: The Psychology of Optimal Experience*, Csikszentmihalyi makes it clear that flow isn't just a wondrous cosmic accident. Flow doesn't just sort of happen when we lay back and do nothing. Flow occurs when we are deeply engrossed in an activity and totally give ourselves to it. It happens when we commit fully to what we are doing, when all of our skills are in play:

> When all a person's relevant skills are needed to cope with the challenges of a situation, that person's attention is completely absorbed by the activity. There is no excess psychic energy left over to process any information but what the activity offers. All the attention is concentrated on the relevant stimuli.

169

As a result, one of the most universal and distinctive features of optimal experience takes place: People become so involved in what they are doing that the activity becomes spontaneous, almost automatic; they stop being aware of themselves as being separate from the actions they are performing.[15]

That last sentence is exquisite, isn't it? When I experience flow I am so absorbed in the moment that I have no time to second-guess myself, to withhold, to doubt. I fully surrender to the unfolding of the moment. I get out of my way. I let go.

THE PROMISES

Here's a final story. The conversation I recount unfurled as I was in the middle of writing this book. In Alcoholics Anonymous they talk about The Promises. The Promises are those small miraculous events that suddenly manifest in people's lives once they have "cleaned up the house." *Infectious* offers you an opportunity to clean up your personal relations house. Consider this story one of The Promises of this book.

It's midday in downtown Chicago, on a sweltering August afternoon. I dash out of the Wyndham Hotel where I have just delivered a workshop and hail a taxi to head to O'Hare Airport. I slide into the back seat and pull the door shut. The cab, as it turns out, is an old Lincoln Mercury that has seen better days. The windows are cracked wide open and the air-conditioning is not on.

Author: *Can we turn on the a/c?*

Driver: *Why don't you move to the front seat?*

I instinctively "get" that it will be easier to cool just the two seats in front of the plexiglas petition. I jump out of the car and plop myself down next to him. The air slowly comes on.

Driver: *You know, your glasses look intimidating.*

He says it to me seconds after I slide into the seat next to him. I look at him for the first time, really, as he utters these words. He's a wiry, dark-skinned man. Short, in his late sixties, I guess. He leans into the steering wheel with a slight hunch as he drives. A jaunty cap twists sideways on his head. He wears glasses, as well—the light, frameless kind.

I am surprised by his comment. Surprised because he said it, and surprised because two nights earlier, I had dinner with my friend Vivian Isaak in Philadelphia, and the topic of my glasses had come up.

Author: *These glasses are a little nerdy. I kind of like that look.*

And then I decide to tell him about my dinner with Vivian.

Author: *I had dinner with a friend in Philadelphia two nights ago. I had not seen her in a couple of years, and she had not seen me with these glasses. She said to me right at the start of dinner "You know, I like these glasses, but you look intimidating in them." Maybe you both are right. Maybe I do look intimidating!*

We banter back and forth about the implications of this coincidence.

Driver: *It's only two comments. This is not statistically valid. The variance is too great.*

I notice that he has a slight accent as he speaks. Accents fascinate me, and his speech reminds me of some of the men I met when I lived in Tobago.

Author: *Where are you from?*

Driver: *My mother's womb.*

I am both amused and annoyed by this answer. I know that I won't settle for this quip of his.

Author: *You know, I lived in Trinidad and Tobago for a while. I don't think you're from there, but I have a hunch you're from somewhere down in the islands.*

Driver: *Guess!*

Author: *I won't guess. Just tell me.*

I hear the irritation in my voice.

Driver: *The Cape Verde Islands. Do you know where they are?*

Author: *I do. Do you know the music of Cesaria Evora?*

Evora is a singer from Cape Verde who has gained a large international following.

Driver: *Yes, I do. So what kind of music do you like?*

I have many answers to that simple question, but I decide to tell him the first thing that comes to mind.

Author: *I like trance and electronic music. I like it because it's mindless and I don't have to think when I listen to it, and it makes me feel good. I have the new Britney Spears CD in my car stereo right now. I listen to it over and over. I think Britney Spears is actually a god-awful singer, but I like this CD. I like all the mindless dance songs on it.*

Driver: *I like classical music and I like jazz.*

Author: *I like that music, too, sometimes.* And then

I remember my other kind of music. *I practice Hinduism. I often go to an ashram in Miami where I meditate and where we chant in Sanskrit. I also love that kind of music.*

He looks at me and says nothing. Drives on in silence. After a pause he responds.

Driver: *I have been meditating for many years. You know, everything in life is about energy. And meditation is a way in which I connect with energy. All of the energy.*

Here's where my heart suddenly seems to skip a beat. My driver has no idea that I am in the middle of writing a book about energetic connections.

Author: *I like chanting in Sanskrit because the words and the chants carry an incredible energy.*

He turns off the classical music station that has been playing.

Driver: *Here's the mantra I chant when I meditate.*

He proceeds to chant for me. It is a low, wailing hum that seems to grow in volume as the sound extends. I notice his deep voice, deeper than his speaking voice, and hear the vibrations in the hum sound. He stops after twenty, twenty-five seconds, at the end of his exhale. And then, as if for emphasis, he chants a second time.

When he is finished we both are silent for a little while.

Driver: *Did you notice the smile on my face when you told me you chant?*

This comment of his makes me smile. I say nothing.

Driver: *There are no accidents in life. I hardly ever ask anybody to sit up front with me. It has been years since*

I have asked anyone to move up.

I glance at him and notice again how wiry his body looks, how he seems to hunch forward with such determination as he drives. He also seems entirely comfortable in his own skin.

Driver: *Most people don't know what is real. They think this car is real. They think these seats are real. They think what they say is real. The true reality is what we discover in the silence.*

I grunt in agreement. I don't know what to add, and I marvel at where he is taking the conversation.

Driver: *Do you ever leave your body?*

Author: *Yes, I have experienced that a bunch of times. I remember having this sense that I, whatever that I is, am hovering high up in the sky, and I am looking down on the room in which I am, and I am watching myself as I am interacting with the people in that room. And I have this strong sense that the part of me that is in the sky is really me, and the person down there in my body is also me.*

Driver: *So you have traveled to the astral planes! Wait till you get to the celestial ones. Some really beautiful things are waiting for you there.*

Our ride continues with stretches of silence interrupted by bursts of chatter. My driver tells me about the time in his life when he began to meditate, over thirty-five years ago. I tell him of my visits to Mother Meera, a spiritual leader from India, and my experience of the darshan ritual with her (darshan is the bestowal of grace by a Hindu holy person to a worshipper). I feel my skin tingle with ripples of energy as we talk. I also feel a great sense of peace, sitting next to him.

As we pull up in front of the United Airlines terminal at O'Hare Airport, I grab my wallet and am surprised that we got here so quickly.

Driver: *I am glad I got to drive you today. You have given me joy for the rest of the day.*

Author: *Thank you for the ride. And thank you so much for the conversation.*

After I pay the fare for this ride, he repeats an earlier comment.

Driver: *And remember. There are no accidents in life.*

I grab my luggage and walk into the terminal.

I don't know my driver's name. I doubt he and I will ever cross paths again. But my moments in the cab ride with him were perfect. We got as close as I think two strangers can get within a twenty-minute conversation.

There were many doors in this conversation. All of them were opened. My driver opened the first one—he commented on my appearance. And he took a risk by opening this door. Because it was a surprising comment, I took notice. I opened the second door by telling him of my conversation with Vivian. The music door turned out to be the path to our common ground. It was the really big common ground, not the "we both like pistachio ice-cream" variety. It was earned common ground—we got there by chatting our way through our different likes in music. It was the door, as it turns out, to something that defines the core of how we both experience the world. How utterly satisfying!

I relish this conversation for another reason: We instantly transcended the roles that came with the social context of this chat—a driver and his passenger. My driver, from the start, disregarded the role conventions by inviting me to sit up front. He immediately violated another convention—engage in social pleasantries—by making a comment about my appearance. This comment might have been perceived as critical or presumptuous. He took a chance. His directness made it easy for me to reach beyond the pleasantries, as well. And off we went.

This was a real conversation, but the roles of driver and passenger are also terrific metaphors for how we navigate in any conversation. A chat between two people is always a drive into the unknown. In a mutually satisfying ride, the roles of driver and passenger are fluid. In any given moment, one of the conversationalists is the driver, the other the passenger. Seconds later, the roles may switch. This shifting of roles becomes the unspoken rhythm of the drive. It causes the ride to accelerate or slow down. It generates excitement, surprise, danger, ennui. A good driver and passenger are attuned to these rhythms. They shift with ease. They notice.

That's where it begins, isn't it? We notice a signal, we notice a hunch, we notice an opportunity. When we notice, things start to happen. When we don't, opportunities slip right past us.

So—I invite you to notice. Drive with grace and stay alert. And whenever possible, steer blissfully into the unknown.

Acknowledgments

Infectious is the result of the immensely gratifying work I get to do, every day. I am greatly indebted to all of you, clients and friends, who allow me and my cohorts at Influens to enter your lives so intimately and engage with you.

Very especially, I wish to express my deep gratitude to:

Tad Crawford and Skyhorse Publishing—for saying yes right away.

Delia Casa—for shepherding this manuscript with such tender care.

Dr. Margarita Gurri—for your indomitable spirit, and for your contributions at the inception of this book, most critically to the book's title and the Power Plugs model.

Donna Ratajzak—for your keen reading of the first draft and your razor-sharp feedback. You have lifted this material to a higher plane!

Irene Borger—for showing up again in my life as the writing kicked into high gear, and for knowing just what to say.

Dan Oropesa—for finding the cover art for this book, for creating the chapter graphics with Thom LaBadia, but most importantly, for running Influens with such unflappable ease.

Leandra Campbell—for crafting the index for this book and "getting it" so quickly.

Kathi Elster—for being my guardian angel from the very start.

Rob Nissen—for helping to spread the word.

My conversation partners—Dr. Isaac Goren, Arnie Kolodner, Melanie Hahn Roche, and Jayne Warrilow—for so generously sharing your wisdom with me.

My associates at Influens—Olga Botcharova, Dr.Robert Hernandez, Carolyn Holland, and Zachary Minor—for pouring yourselves into the work with such commitment and skill.

My angels in the business world—Marci Bloch, Elaine McRae, Tina Governo, Brian Wallace, Kit Williams—for your faith in what we offer.

Philip Friday—for your unwavering friendship and support during the writing of this book.

Flash Maroncelli—for reminding me of how energy is channeled.

Mother Meera—for sending the light.

Ane—my mother—for loving me as I am.

And The Chromatics—for making music that loops to the past and leaps to the future.

About the Author

ACHIM NOWAK is an internationally recognized authority on executive presence and infectious personal connections. His first book, *Power Speaking: The Art of the Exceptional Public Speaker,* has become an essential leadership development tool in Fortune 500 companies around the world. Achim has coached hundreds of executives and entrepreneurs. He integrates an extensive background in personal transformation techniques, conflict resolution, spiritual practice, and actor training to develop resonant leaders.

Influens, the international training and coaching firm Achim founded in 2004, is based in South Florida. It has guided thousands of leaders from organizations such as Sanofi, Dover Corporation, HSBC Bank, Blue Cross/Blue Shield, and City of Miami Beach to better connect and be more influential. From training performers at the Actors Institute to leading transformational seminars in AIDS communities throughout North America, from directing an Israeli/Palestinian theater production for the Peres Center for Peace to windsurfing in Tobago for a year and doing absolutely nothing—Achim has mastered the art of slipping in and out of any social setting.

Achim holds an M.A. in organizational psychology and international relations from New York University. He served for over a decade on the faculty of New York University and has been a frequent guest speaker at other universities such as the University of Massachusetts, Amherst College, Brandeis University, and Columbia University.

Achim's writing has appeared in leading industry magazines and numerous anthologies. He has been recognized with a PEN Syndicated Fiction Award. Achim and his work have been featured on *60 Minutes, The Today Show*, NPR, HLN, and in the award-winning documentary *The Last Enemy.* When he is not traveling or coaching, Achim enjoys the simple pleasures of the South Florida beach life.

www.influens.com

Notes

1. Alex "Sandy" Pentland, *Honest Signals: How They Shape Our World* (Cambridge: MIT Press, 2008).

2. Alex "Sandy" Pentland, "Defend Your Research: We Can Measure the Power of Charisma" (Harvard Business Review, January 2010).

3. Pew Research Center's Internet & American Life Project (accessed March 12, 2012). http://www.pewinternet.org.

4. Adam Bryant, "Don't Ask 'How Are You?' Unless You Mean It" (*New York Times*, November 28, 2009).

5. Anthony Robbins, *Giant Steps: Small Changes to Make a Big Difference* (New York: Touchstone Publishing, 1994), 190.

6. Mike Nichols, "Julia Opens Up to Mike Nichols" (Vanity Fair, April 2012), 174.

7. Marianne Faithfull, and David Dalton, *Faithfull: An Autobiography* (New York: Cooper Square, 2000), 42.

8. "Charisma." In The New Oxford American Dictionary, eds. Angus Stevenson and Christine A. Lindberg (New York: Oxford University Press, 2010).

9. John Potts, *A History of Charisma.* (Basingstoke: Palgrave Mac-Millan, 2009), 2.

10. Zachary Woolfe, "A Gift from the Musical Gods" (New York Times, August 21, 2011).

11. Erving Goffman, *The Presentation of Self in Everyday Life* (London: Penguin, 1990), 28.

12. Carl Jung, video, "Carl Gustav Jung on Kundalini (full story)" (video, 8:42, March 29, 2012). www.youtube.com/watch?v=rMr3X_60h_Q.

13. "What Makes George Run" (TDF Stages, January 2008).

14. George Leonard, *Mastery: The Keys to Success and Long-Term Fulfillment* (New York: Plume, 1991), 141.

15. Mihalyi Csikszentmihalyi. *Flow: The Psychology of Optimal Experience* (New York: Harper Perennial, 2008), 53.

Index